College Memories and Other Rimes

Much of Which has appeared before in

THE COLORADO COLLEGE TIGER

「大学の思い出」
と
その他の詩

ウィリアム・メレル・ヴォーリズ 著

畠中　康男 訳

英宝社

ウィリアム・メレル・ヴォーリズ氏
（コロラド・カレッジ卒業時の肖像）

ティクノー館の旧館
（1897-1898 年建築当時の写真）

ティクノー館の新館

カトラー館
（1915 年頃に撮影）

カトラー館正面

ショーヴ記念礼拝堂

カレッジ学生たちの園遊会風景

著者自身の筆による油絵「松ノ木林」
（公益財団法人近江兄弟社ヴォーリズ記念館所蔵）

College Memories and Other Rimes

MUCH OF WHICH HAS
APPEARED BEFORE IN

THE COLORADO COLLEGE TIGER

BY

WM. MERRELL VORIES,
of the Class of 1904

———

"A little nonsense, now and then,
Is relished by the wisest men."

———

PUBLISHED BY SUBSCRIPTION,1903

PREFATORY NOTE

Written chiefly for diversion and never honored with revision, the following *doggerel* is not, and does not claim to be, *literature*–let us save criticism's breath in advance. Very probably the perpetrator himself will look back upon it in years to come with anything but satisfaction.

The first piece, which lends its name to the collection, may be taken as typical of the whole: -Three parts *nonsense*, to one where sense is attempted (and which, for that very reason, will probably appear to the reader most ridiculous).

Yet, punctured though it be so thickly with faults that it resembles more the sieve than the chalice, it still goes forth with the hope that somewhere there may cling within it a drop of cheer, perhaps even a stray, suggested flavor of something higher, or at least, an atom of tonic against the, "*blues*" and dyspepsia.

Many thanks are due, and are heartily given, the friends who by encouragement, assistance, and subscriptions have made this little book possible, and to them it is gratefully dedicated.

W. M. V.

Colorado College, Colorado Springs, May, 1903.

CONTENTS

FRONTISPIECE – "The Pines" — from an oil paint by the author.

1. College Memories ···1
2. Reuben Strawstack at the Banquet ·····················6
3. A Nervous Reflex ··18
4. Ticknor Hall ··21
5. "Strike While the Iron is Hot" ·······················23
6. Rough on Dutch ···25
7. The Real Dutch ··26
8. Truth ··27
9. The Cow ···28
10. A Valentine ··29
11. A Desperate Situation (or The Easter Bonnet) ······31
12. May 26, 1902 ···33
13. On a Basket Ball Poster ····································35
14. The Equinoxial Storm ·······································36
15. Et tu, Avis? ···37
16. A Thanksgiving Nightmare ································39
17. The Other Point of View ···································42
18. The Error and the Wrong ·································43
19. The Mountain and the Seasons ···························44
20. Anemones ···49
21. The Anemone ···50
22. The Pines ···51
23. To Spenser (A Sonnet) ······································52
24. To Byron (A Sonnet) ··53
25. On Friendship (A Sonnet) ··································54
26. To D. C. M. ··55

27. The Strenuous Life ·······································56
28. Gold or A Human Life ······························57
29. "With Trembling Hands Uplift" ·······················59
30. The Christmas Gift ································60
31. A Prayer ······································63

1. COLLEGE MEMORIES.

I.

I remember, I remember the night before exam,—
The flick'ring midnight candle that lighted up my *cram*,
The blurring page before me, the towel 'round my head,
The doleful striking of the hours, as I sat there and read
Through many a stranger volume, and unsoiled pages
       turned,
And tried to learn the learning that erst I should have
      learned.

I remember, I remember the room in which 'twas held,—
The rows of anxious faces of students strangely quelled;
The maze of hieroglyphics chalked thickly o'er the board,
With *Question-points*, like demons, that seemed extending
      toward
The victims scornful fingers, and at our fright to scoff;
And, like some nightmare monster, the terrifying *prof.*

I remember, I remember, but here my mem'ry fails,
(My over-burdened brain-cells refused to hold details).
Unconsciously I scribbled, my mind with cramming drunk;
I have no notion whether *condition*, *pass*, or *flunk*
Will mark the doubtful answers my aching brain produced:

1

I only know exams. are o'er—and *I was not excused.*

II.

I remember, I remember those Canon picnics gay
Which chaperoned co-edites enjoyed each holiday,—
The hay-rides in the moonlight, the hay-ricks that broke
      down,
The clearing of the wreckage, the weary walk to town;
The delicate refreshments, abbreviated, cold,
With more of bread and butter than thirty hogs could hold,—

Till piles of good sandwiches went ruthlessly to waste,—
And scarce enough confections to get a decent taste;
And how the bramble bushes inflicted us with scratches!
And how the bugs and beetles conducted swimming
      matches
In lemonade and milk pails! And how the busy ants
Essayed to steal the sugar, and in the butter dance!

I remember, I remember the glorious mountain climbs,
More hard upon the suff'ring *feet* than are these wretched
      rimes;
How horse-back rides relieved us when language roads
      were rough!
How ill-learned recitations drove us to Austin's *Bluff!*

COLLEGE MEMORIES

And when examination had flunked us all, *en masse*,
How longingly we cast our eyes upon the great Ute *Pass!*

III.

I remember, I remember how at the Barbecue,
Without a wing to aid me, high through the air I flew,—
The singing and speech-making, the beef and pumpkin pie,
The pickles and the cider, peanuts and apples by
The hundred,—all these good things seem little more than
  dross
When measured by the pleasures that crown the Blanket-
  toss.

I remember, I remember the upturned faces there,
A hundred feet beneath me as I sail'd through the air;
The bird s-eye panorama, the bonfire's little spark
That flickered far below me, a beacon in the dark;
The swift descent and landing, and then another flight:—
I tell you, Blanket-tossing is simply *out of sight!*

I remember, I remember the far-famed Pearsons Goat,—
The night his fearful horny head upon my person smote;
His strong, sonorous bleating that to my trembling ear
Seemed like approaching cyclones, and shook my frame
  for fear;

College Memories and Other Rimes

The vigor of his bucking, his energetic butt,
Outstripped the strongest slugger's most mighty upper-cut!

IV.

I remember, I remember—my heart warms at the thought—
The friendships, true and tender, that to my life have
  brought
Bright rays of hope's pure sunshine when threat'ning storms
  assailed;
True friends, whose love and loyalty and confidence ne'er
  failed—
Though other men might doubt me and deem my motives
  wrong—
And yet who never cheated me with flattery's false tongue;

True friends, who shared my struggles through bright and
  cloudy days,
Sincere in helpful counsel as careful in their praise;
Whose friendship was not founded on selfishness or jest,
But, seeing good and ill in me, strove to upbuild the best;
True friends—ah, yes, how could I resent, as once I did,
The honest criticism 'neath which their love was hid!

I remember, I remember with gratitude the debt
I owe these men whose counsel has kept me from the net

COLLEGE MEMORIES

Of carelessness or narrowness of living and of thought—
And this I hold the lesson their type of friendship taught:
True friends are those who help one to gain his noblest end,
And he *must* be a helper who *would* be a true friend.

College Memories and Other Rimes

2. REUBEN STRAWSTACK AT THE BANQUET.

(Dedicated to Pearson's Literary Society.)

I wuz lately on a visit
Tew—By cracky! naow—whar is it?
O, yes—Coloraddy College,
Whar they feed their *minds* on knowledge,
An' the *rest* uv 'em with eatin'
Thet is mighty hard uv beatin'.
I wuz thar tew see my cousin,
(Guess I've got about a dozen—
But I mean the sorter witty
One thet grow'd up in the city),
Who belongs tew a sas-si-ty
Thet wuz givin' uv a mighty
Monstrous banquet on the night
I wuz thar. He 'lowed 'twas right
Fur tew take *me*; so I went
Without diggin' up a cent!

Wall, the weather it wuz mild
Ez a little, sleepin' child;
Not a cloud wuz in the skies;
Yew could almost hear the rise

6

REUBEN STRAWSTACK AT THE BANQUET

Uv the spring-proclaimin' sap
In the trees, whose winter nap,
Drowsy-like, wuz almost over;
Here an' thar a patch uv clover
Wuz a-greenin'; an' the singin'
Uv the early birds wuz ringin',
Till the air all wavey trembled
Through an' through, till it resembled
Ripplin' water; an' the breezes
Had thet earthy scent which seizes
Yew with curiousest longin's,
(Whether they air right or wrong uns)
Jest tew drap yer bizness, givin'
Up yerself tew simply livin'.

Yes, I give in tew his urgin',
An' decided on emergin'
In a rented full-dress suit—
(Gosh, be blamed! It wuz a *beaut!*)
An' the fellers interduced me
Tew the gal they'd picked fer me,
An' they didn't have ter boost me
Few she suited tew a T.

Wall, we got thar close tew eight,
But we hed a spell tew wait;

7

College Memories and Other Rimes

So it must-a bin 'bout nine
When they formed us into line.
Then we marched down, two by two,
From the settin'-room an' through
Whar the office-boys an' guests
  Wuz lined up tew watch us pass,—
(Thar they set an' cracked their jests;
  Looked tew me like powerful sass!)
Daown into the *Dinin' Hall*.—
Did ye ast ef it wuz *small?*
Wall, by cracky! I should figger
It wuz jest 'bout ten times bigger
Thun the meetin' house tew home,
Not a-countin' in the dome.
An' the walls wuz jest ez red
Ez Ol' Tompkin's milkin' shed,
Or the row uv hollyhocks
'Tween the pasture an' the rocks
By the crick; 'twas powerful bright;
An' the floor wuz *paved* an' *white!*
An' thet hundred-foot-long table—
Wall, by Ned! I jest aint able
Fer tew give the least idee
Uv the way it looked tew me.
It wuz wide as *ourn* is long,—
If I don't remember wrong, —

REUBEN STRAWSTACK AT THE BANQUET

An' jest loaded down with posies,—
Front uv every gal wuz roses,—
An' long lines uv smilax, viney-
Like, wound all around the chiney.

Like matched oxen in their yokes,
We wuz paired with women folks;
Ev'ry feller hed beside him
Some pert female tew divide him
'Twixt her clever talk a-heedin'
An' attendin' tew the feedin'.
Uv these gals they wuz 'bout thirty,
An' my pardner wuz ez purty
Ez the next un. I'll jest bet yer
Mighty few uv 'em could tetch her;—
Real uncommon handsome lookin',
(Doubt ef she'd be much at cookin')
Sorter whitish han's an' face;
Wore a sight uv frills an' lace.
An' she talked ez interestin'
An' ez chipper ez the best 'un
'Bout the weather an' the flowers—
Never tired the hull four hours.
She hed monstrous talkin' powers!
Yes, she wus about the pick
Uv the bunch—I see thet quick.

College Memories and Other Rimes

Wall, in front uv each one's plate
Stood a order card with great
Soundin' eatables stuck on't,
Like a reg'lar restaurant.
I wuz doubtful what we'd strike,
So I sez, un-ruffled-like,
Tew the waiter by my chair:
"Fetch the hull blamed *billy-fare!*"
"*Das jes' what we gwine ter do!*"
Sez he, laughin', soz I knew
He wuz a good-nater'd cuss,
An' not apt tew raise a fuss.

Such a sight uv eatin' tools!
  Knives an' forks an' spoons, a pile,
An' they used 'em all by rules
  Which the same wuz set by *style*,
So I ast my pardner's views
As tew which uv 'em tew use
First. She sed "*From outside in*"
Wuz the order she hed bin
Told tew foller.—(Naow, *I* say
Thet yer *bound* tew eat thet way!)

REUBEN STRAWSTACK AT THE BANQUET

Soon ez we wuz settled well,
Here come oysters in the shell;
An' the pesky little suckers
Stuck like corn-husks when the shuckers
Tew a huskin' bee is burstin
Almost, tryin' tew be first 'un
Tew git done. The very worst 'un
I give up, half out the shell,
Jest ez they hed rung the bell
Fer tew take the plates away—
(Hardest work I'd done thet day!)
Next the coffee cups wuz brought,
(Least thet's what I really thought),
Full uv nicest coffee, hot
Ez the fire beneath the pot.
Careful-like I picked it up,
Filled the sasser from the cup,
Swallered some,—an' raised a whoop—
Fer the thing wuz filled with soup!
Soup in coffee-cups, by thunder!
Wuzn't thet a *awful* blunder!—
'Spose with sech a pack uv souls
They wuz sorter shy uv bowls.

Then thy fetched a mess uv fish
Thet wuz good ez ye could wish;

College Memories and Other Rimes

Only naow an' then a bone
Made yew wish yew wuz alone.

Next things up wuz listed "Patties";—
Naow, perhaps *yew* know what *that* is:
Little round things filled with stew,
Like a little pot uv glue.
Wall, I stuck my spoon into it,
But I cuddent shove it through it,
Fer the thing wuz made uv paper!
Naow warn't thet a cur'ous caper?—
I hev heared that off tew school
They feed paper *April Fool;*
But a banquet aint no place
Fer tew act up in sech ways!

Then they fetched suthin' tew drink—
Circus lemonade, I think.
It wuz nice an' red an' sweet,
An' its taste wuz hard tew beat;
Only it hed not bin strained,
So thet, when yet glass wuz drained,
Little chunks uv fruit remained,
Or got in yer mouth an' choked
Yer, jest as yer gal had joked,
An' yew felt jest about half

12

REUBEN STRAWSTACK AT THE BANQUET

Like ye'd bust unless ye'd laugh.
Punch they called this drinkin' mess;
An' the reason is, I guess,
'Coz yew hev ter *punch* away
Bits uv fruit thet block the way.
But it bein' powerful good,
Things like thet wuz easy stood.

In sev'ral way I liked the most
The little quails they fetched on toast.
They wuz the purtiest lookin' sight,
Not countin' gals, I seen thet night;
But awful tough!—I would hev 'lowed
Mine wuz the gran-dad uv the crowd.

Bird-meat wuz a favor-ite
With the hull of us thet night.
After they hed tuck the bones
Uv the quails tew kitchen zones,
Chicken salad wuz the next
Thet our stummick regions vext.
I'd hev et my scraps uv hen
Better ef the gravey'd ben
Not so sour. But then this balk
Give the chance tew stop an' talk.
I wuz gettin' purty full,

College Memories and Other Rimes

Anyhow, so in the lull,
Turnin' tew my gal, I ast:
"How much longer duz this last?"
"Wall," she sez, "I reckon soon
It'll stop—thar's jest a spoon
Left unused, an' I shud guess
That'd finish up the mess."

Wall, however that might seem,
Next thing give us wuz *Ice Cream,*
(Thet's my fav'rit kinder sass.)
  It wuz white, but full uv real
Cur'ous little chunks like glass,
  With the taste uv citron peel.

Thar wuz cakes uv ev'ry style
Settin' 'round, pile after pile;
An', soz not tew be behind,
I tuck some uv ev'ry kind—
Though it almost stretched me blind!

But the *fruit*, piled up invitin'
'Long the table, we wuz slightin'.
Not a one hed et a grape
Or a orange, or no shape
Uv the fruit; so I sez, quiet

14

REUBEN STRAWSTACK AT THE BANQUET

To my gal: "Say, les us try it."
"I'm too full," she sez, "les knock it
   Off the program." I replied:
"Chuck a apple in yer pocket,—
   Yew kin eat it then outside!"

Jest then, right at the tail end,
What shud thet hotel man send
But *real* coffee, sure enough—
This time 'twant no *soup* er bluff!
Ev'rything wuz rattlin' good:
I et jest the best I cud—
But thar wuz *one* thing thet I
Cuddent do ef I shud try
Till the end uv kingdom come;
   That wus break the *"Water Crackers"*.—
Tried until my hands wuz numb!
  But I guess some careless packers
In the fact'ry must-a sot 'em
Whar they afterwards fergot 'em;
An' they must-a stood fer years,
  Till they got so hard an' dry
Thet they'd bust a pair uv shears.
  So, when no one seemed to spy,
I jest slipped one tew the floor
(Which wuz clean I see before),

College Memories and Other Rimes

An' by trompin' with my heel
Broke it up, quite a good deal.
Then I knocked a spoon off quick,
Soz thar'd be a chance tew pick
Up the pieces I hed broke,
An' give 'em a while tew soak
In the coffee, till they'd thawed
Soft enough soz to be chawed.

O, yes, I came nigh not a-sayin'
How they kep' a band a-playin'
All the time we wuz at dinner;
An' it wuzn't no beginner,
But a real professional crowd—
Didn't play tew soft ner loud,
But jest thet sorter dreamy way
That makes the hull year seem like May;
Thet kinder oozy-woozy sound,
Like angel pinions flappin' 'round;
So thet the talkin' wuzn't drown'd,
But with the tune seemed tew be wound.

'Bout the time we'd got plumb done,
  These band fellers up an' went;
Then commenct some diff'rent fun;
  Makin' speeches pert, thet sent

16

REUBEN STRAWSTACK AT THE BANQUET

Waves uv laughin' surgin' 'round,
Like a rabbit with a hound
Chasin' uv it. I'll be bound
I aint *never* laughed before
Half so much. Why, I wuz *sore*
From a-laughin'! After that,
I aint certain jest where at,
Thar wuz four young fellers sang.
Then the hall with clappin' rang,
An' they sang one more, er two—
Lots uv noise, fer sech a few,—
An' 'twuz powerful purty, tew!
Wall, sir, I lost track uv time.
I'd hev sold out fer a dime
When I seen, when we wuz done,
It wuz awful clost tew *one!*
Street cars wuz put up fer night;
But the moon wuz shinin' bright,
An' we hed a right smart sight
More uv talk an' laughin', too,
Walkin' home thar, tew by tew.

An' I've bin thinkin' ever sence:
These bloomin' banquets is immense!

3. A NERVOUS REFLEX.

(Dedicated to the Psychology A Class.)

"On old Moriah's piny tops
A Finn and German picked some hops."
This simple verse was given to me
To help me learn anatomy.
My *Auditory* caught the sound
And sent reflexes surging round.
And first th' *Abducent* nerve contracted,
Then *Motor-Oculi* reacted.
The eye-ball slowed up with a jerk
And let the *Optic* do its work.—
Thus memory was aided quite
A little by the sense of sight.

The *Glosso* and *Olfactory*
Were stirred up out of sympathy.
Through *Facial* and *Trifacial*, too,
The sensitive reflexes flew.
And down my *Pneumo-Gastric* thrilled
The shock, until my blood was chilled.
Upon my hands my head fell cold,—
The *Spinal* nerve had ceased to hold;
So shocked it was by this refrain

A NERVOUS REFLEX

It bent like rubber 'neath the strain,
But worst of these effects colossal
Was that upon my *Hypo-Glossal.*

This nerve began to vibrate so
My tongue like lightning 'gan to go:
" *'On old Moriah's'*—one, two, three,—
Olfactory, Optic, Oculi!
'On old Moriah's piny top'—
Patheticus, Trifacial,—stop!
Enough of this !"—yet on I went:
" *'A Finn and German' —Abducent,*
Facial and Auditory, Gloss-
O! This is making me quite cross!—
They *'Picked Some'*—Vague (or Pneumo)—
Yes, that's the way it ought to go!—

" *'Some'*—Spinal — er—Accessory;
'Hops'—Hypo-Glossal—Let me see—
Ah! That is all!"—But, horrors!—then
My reflexed tongue begins again!
So all day long, against my will,
Reflexes keep me mumbling still:
"On old Moriah's piny tops,
A Finn and German Picked some hops."
Now, as I daily suffer thus,

19

College Memories and Other Rimes

Am I not a *Pathetic Cuss?*

4. TICKNOR HALL.

Song.—(*Tune*: "*Forsaken.*")

I.

It stands on the campus the queen of the Halls;
What fancies, what memories breathe round its walls,
Its drawing-room, dining-room, corridors, hall—
And its study, its *study!*—round *it* most of all!

II.

Whenever we enter at Ticknor we seem
Surrounded by spirits as if in a dream;
And they whisper strange stories of pleasures of yore,
Of class celebrations and functions galore.

III.

For at Ticknor the *co-eds* their citadel hold;
And not half of its secrets have ever been told.
We hear of their *Fudges*, their *Rare-bits*, and such,
But, compared with the facts, what we know is not much.

College Memories and Other Rimes

IV.

So we dream and we listen to the tales of the elves
Of past celebrations like the ones we ourselves
Have shared in, and laughed o'er, and will ever recall,
While we hold in fond mem'ry our belov'd Ticknor Hall.

5. "STRIKE WHILE THE IRON IS HOT."

Now Greek is a terror,
  And Latin's a fright,
    And Spanish is really too much;
But unless I'm in error,
 There's nothing that's quite
  As awful to tackle as Dutch.
    Two hours on Italian,
      A half more for French,
        Will usually do; but for Dutch,
      From a student battalion
        To a judge on the bench,
          A day and a half's not too much.
Ten students together
 Might work for ten hours,
   (A hundred straight hours for one such);
And yet I doubt whether,
 Combining their powers,
   They'd manage to get out their Dutch.
     Then rouse ye, my brothers,
       "In union there's strength"
         United by sympathy's touch,
       Let's strike with the others
         Against the great length

College Memories and Other Rimes

Of these terrible lessons in *Dutch*:

6. ROUGH ON DUTCH.

(And, Incidentally, on Tennyson.)

Dutch! Dutch! Dutch!
  When I meditate on thee,
My tongue would scarce dare utter
  The thoughts that arise in me!

Plug, plug, plug!
  'Tis the same old tune always,
With never a rest from grinding,
  Not a cut or a holiday!

And the suff'ring class goes down
  To the *Obs*, on the side of the hill;
But O, for the joy of a vanquished prof.,
  And a classroom hushed and still!

7. THE REAL DUTCH.

You can say what you please about *Dutch*
  It takes ten hours a day, we'll admit;
But for training few courses can touch
  Diese Sprache—und fertig damit!

For each hour of our sweat-shoppish toil
  Spent in getting our translations well,
There's a soothing and pain-killing oil
  Wann scherzt unser Lehrer so hell!

More of work, more of fun, less of waste,
  In the time which we spend in pursuit
Of this language of culture and taste:—
  Und ein thaetiges Leben 'st sehr gut!

8. TRUTH.

One time a fool
Was sent to school
To learn some sense
And clear the dense
Delusion from
His cranium;
This is no lie:
That fool was I.

9. THE COW.

The cow is a gentle creature,
  She stands as still as death;
With peace perched in each feature
  And Sen-Sen scented breath.

Her cloak is soft and silky,
  And smooth and shiny, too;
Her teeth are white and milky,
  Her horns are navy blue.

Her legs are long and graceful, —
  More graceful than a calf's;
Her mouth is quite a faceful
  As often as she laughs.

But still one vulgar habit
  Nips beauty in the bud;
Like high-school girl and rabbit,
  She's always chewing cud.

10.   A VALENTINE.

A gentle breeze
Stirs in the trees,
　Stars twinkle in the sky;
The woodland way
Alone I stray;
　Would thou, my love, wert nigh!

I see thy face,
Thy features trace,
　In every cloud-decked sky;
"Come back to me,
I long for thee!"
　The lapping wavelets cry.

I hear the sound
Of merry round
　Of song and mirth afar;
But without thee
All sounds to me
　Are sadly off the *tar*—

(I mean the *pitch*—
The stuff of which
　The former's made, they say.)

College Memories and Other Rimes

But, wo is me!
I feel no glee,
  For thou art far away!

11. A DESPERATE SITUATION.

(Or The Easter Bonnet.)

The other day I saw so strange a bonnet,
That, quite amazed, I sat me down upon it
To write some jingling verse or stately sonnet.
I do not mean, now, mind you, I'm explaining,
That on the *hat* I sat me down, remaining
While from the Muse the inspiration gaining;
But on a chair I sat me down, with pencil—
('Tis true, I might have used a pen; but when will
A pen become so useful a utensil?)
Nor do I mean that on the hat the writing
Should be inscribed; for graphite in uniting
With millinery foliage might be blighting
It was on sweetly-scented, *ink-lined* paper
I sat me down beside my burning taper
To execute for you this rhythmic caper.
But now I see again I've blurred my meaning,
As if upon the *inclined* paper I'd been leaning:—
I seem possessed my purpose to keep screening!
I sat me down, as I have just been saying,
My plans for rhythmic lines minutely laying,
And all my verbous store-house nicely weighing.
—I started out to write abou a bonnet

College Memories and Other Rimes

That had a wondrous jungle growing on it;
But now I find I really haven't done it!

Envoy

Once criticisms scarcely beatific
Were hurled at me for being un-specific;
This time I hope for comments more pacific.

12.   MAY 26, 1902.

For hours it dripped
From the cloud-filled sky
As if by some guy
 The tank were tipped.
            The roads ran rivers,
            The rivers ran floods;
            Through the spring-dressed buds,
             Ran watery shivers.

 A new-set tree
In the campus park,
For want of an ark
 In which to flee,
            Was washed ten feet
            From its starting place,
            And sailed with the grace
             Of a modern fleet!

 But worst of all,
In a goodly line,
The Co-Eds who dine
 At Ticknor Hall
            Across Cascade,
            With its rushing tide
            Nearly twelve feet wide,
             Dared not to wade.

College Memories and Other Rimes

'Neath scanty cover,
Dripping, stood these same,
Till four brave youth came
And helped them over.

13.   ON A BASKET BALL POSTER.

Now, once again, we hear the call
Inviting us to Basket Ball.
The Seniors and the Sophomores,
Amid the crowd's excited roars,
Will play the Junior-Freshman team!
The gym—aglare with 'lectric gleam,
And warm as toast with stewing steam,—
Will open to receive the stream
Of students, Thursday night, 'twould seem;
And from the sideline seats the cream
Of fair co-eds will sweetly beam,—
Each cheering for her own class team.
To miss this stirring, grand event
Would be to give the notion vent
That you have not a single cent;
For who has sense can't be prevent-
Ed following up the Basket scent.
Since *two* can go for twenty-five,
But *one* is fifteen, all should strive
To bring a partner—for to thrive
And get ahead in life will drive
A man to save his senses five.

College Memories and Other Rimes

14. THE EQUINOXIAL STORM.

'Twas on the morn of March eleventh,
(Just four short days after the seventh),
That in the dim, uncertain light
I saw a strange and savage sight,
  Which made my blood run cold.

Around the flag-pole, ('though 'twas chill)
On which they'd pasted up a bill
Which aimed to squelch the Freshman class,
The Soph'more girls kept watch, *en masse,*
  With threat'ning mien, and bold.

A Freshman delegation fair,
Approached with Carrie-Nation air.
Attack was met with stern rebuff;
The thing became a little rough—
  And foes began to mix.

Ah! Never was a stranger scene!
Perplexed, I cried: "What does this mean?"
Was it a scene from Dante's *Hades?*
No; just a scrap between the ladies
  Of Naughty-Five and –'Six.

15. ET TU, AVIS?

Once strolling through Birdvill, I happened to see
A queer advertisement high up in a tree:
"Instructions in flying by J. Bird, Esquire,
Professional winger and famous high-flyer."
I stood all amazed, for I always had thought.
That nestlings should be by their own parents taught.
So I asked an old owl in a neighboring pine
What the meaning might be of that strange-sounding sign.
Quoth she: "In our city we have female clubs.—
A bear shouldn't give all her time to her cubs!—
Congenial companions in clubs flock together,
(You call it a *clique*—we call it a *feather*),
To discuss weighty matters—like fashions in plumes,
('Tis immensely more pleasant than searching old brooms
For nest-straw, to make better homes in our nation!)
We have a most prosperous Association
Of Musical Talent, both players and singers;
And we're getting to be most astonishing wingers
In our Soaring Society. Once every week
We all fly together around that high peak.

In politics, too, of our bird-commonwealth,
And in matters pertaining to diet and health,
(The best kinds of beetles for breakfast and dinner,

The fact—all unknown to the unlearned beginner—
That germs and bacteria and such fearful pests
Inhabit the rubbish we once used for nest!
Till we've taken to using, instead, only straw
Disinfected by officers under the law;
And some of our prominent germ-agitators
Have urged us for nests to employ incubators)—
In such deep researches the mother bird delves;
But the tender young nestlings aren't left by themselves,
Oh, no! we hire nurse-birds to watch night and day,
While we are on *matters of moment* away.
And when it comes time for the young things to fly,
W send for J. Bird, whose sign you espy.
From the nest *he* can *push* them as well as can we;—
(And, really, he charges a moderate fee!)"
I heard, and was struck with profoundest dismay.
It seemed as if Nature were run to decay.
The trees drooped in sorrow; as if in a shroud,
The mountain peak covered his face with a clound;
And the heavens, in sympathy over earth's pain,
Dropped gently upon her the tears if their rain.—
I opened my lips to protest with owl,
But she laughed me to scorn, and replied, with a scowl:
"'Tis *Civilization* has taught us the plan;
We once were all pagans—we now mimic *Man*."

16. A THANKSGIVING NIGHTMARE.

(Apologies to Fitz-Greene Halleck.)

At midday in the oven warm,
  The turk lay dreaming of the hour
When guests, who'd braved the blinding storm,
  'Neath branching palm and flower,
Would with the host and hostess share
The plentiful Thanksgiving fare,
In dreams, he saw the goup's glad gaze
  Beam on his brown-baked breast,
  And, proudest bird in east or west,
  He heard the appetiteful guest
His ponderous plumpness praise.
An hour passed on—the turk awoke;
  That bright dream was his last;
He woke—to hear clear bell-taps call
The feasters to the dining hall,
He woke—in presence of these folk,
To fall beneath the carver's stroke,
  By thrust of steel harassed.

Before th' assembled eyes there came
A dinner worthy of the name,
  A table crown'd with cheer.

39

Fruits from the forest and the field,
Stacked till the staunch board fairly reel'd,
Ev'rything tooth-some harvests yield
    They saw in plenty here.

They ate like sarved men, long and well:
    They stuffed their stomachs—each his own;
They conquered—and the turkey fell,
    All but the bare-picked bone.
And many a well-timed yarn was spun,
As mastication raced with fun;—
    And the great feast was o'er.
That eyening, late, saw eyelids close
O'er feaster's eyes, who sought repose,
    And, seeking, paced the floor.

Come to the slumber-chamber, Sleep!
    Come to the feaster when he feels
For the first time, he's gorged too deep;
    Come when his hot brain reels!
At midnight, in the chamber's chill,
    The sleepless folk could not keep still,
But tossed in troubled, tortured dreams
    Of stalking barnyards filled with fowl,
    Of fruits and nuts and bubbling bowl,
Of pies and pudding, cakes and creams.

A THANKSGIVING NIGHTMARE

Now phantom gobblers scoff at each,
  And pluri-peded pumpkin pies,
In ominous tones their lessons teach
  To each sick sufferer, where he lies,
Full late into the wee small hours
The conquerors feel the conquered's powers;
In wakeful dreams, they hear this taunt:
  "My dear, kind friends, be of good cheer,
  Thanksgiving comes but once a year,
So eat all that you want!"

College Memories and Other Rimes

17. THE OTHER POINT OF VIEW.

Lives of bums and drunks remind us,
  We can make a hit while here,
And, departing, leave behind us,
  Scents of cigarettes and beer.

Odors that perhaps another,
  Setting out to be a swell,
Some forlorn, lightheaded brother,
  May start on the road to hell.

18. THE ERROR AND THE WRONG.

(With Apologies to Longfellow)

I shot an *Error* into the air,
It fell to earth, I did not care;
For, so thoughtless I'd grown, the sight
Of ill-wrought work caused me no fright.

I breathed a *Wrong* into the air,
It fell to earth, I know not where;
For who has insight keen and strong
Enough to trace the results of Wrong?

Long, long afterward, far and wide,
I found the *Error* multiplied;
And the *Wrong*, by some boomerang art,
I found returning had pierced my own heart.

College Memories and Other Rimes

19. THE MOUNTAIN AND THE SEASONS.

I.

Like a sentry, stands the mountain,
  Guarding field and wood and plain,
Through the changing scenes and seasons,
  In the sunshine, in the rain.
First to greet the morning sunbeam,
  Last to lose the sinking ray,
While in haze of dawn or twilight
  Plains and valleys round him lay,
He has stood, and standeth ever;
For he leaves his watching never.

II.

When he sees the harvests garnered,
  Feels the biting Autumn blast,
When the chilling hoar-frost gathers,
  And the Summer's reign is past,—
Then he wraps his rugged shoulders
  In his autumn mantle gay,
Like the storied coat of Joseph
  In its many-hued display;

For its beauty naught surpasses,
Wrought of tinted leaves and grasses.

III.

But when Winter, hard and heartless,
  Striking wildly right and left,
Blasting with his cruel coldness,
  Like some being sense-bereft
Seems to ruthlessly determine
  All the earth with death to smite,—
In a robe of richest ermine,
  Diamond-studded, sparkling bright,
Scornfully the Mountain warms him,
And the blizzard never harms him.

IV.

Then comes bud-engend'ring Springtime,
  Setting valleys in array,
All their winter bleakness rend'ring
  Verdant in new garments gay.
And the Mountain, seeing round him
  All these fresh-apparelled folk,
Calls to Nature quick to weave him
  A more seasonable cloak:

College Memories and Other Rimes

For his winter coat is fading,
And its weight his shoulders lading.

V.

So dame Nature on her world-loom
  Doth begin to weave and spin
For the Mountain's summer costume,
  With rich stuffs of varied green.
Hark, the sounds of busy humming!
  Though 'tis said her work is still,
Hear her schuttle in the brooklet's
  Babble and the songster's trill.
With the birds' first notes beginning,
Nature sets her looms a-spinning.

VI.

Wondrous is the new creation!
  Step by step from base to height,
As the melting snow-line rises
  Higher, higher, day and night,—
To its very border pressing,
  Climbs the summer fabric, green,
Dotted rich with wild-flower beading,
  Standing forth in glorious sheen;

46

Till at length from plain to summit
It has spread, in art consumate.

VII.

With each shifting of the shadows
  As the hours of day progress,
Every glen and dome and turret
  Takes on added loveliness,
From the halo of the morning
  Till the ev'ning sun goes down,
Leaving shafts of gold and crimson
  For that last transcendent crown;
And the summer moor shines brightly,
Adding varied beauties nightly.

VIII.

Thus unchanged, yet ever changing,
  Stands the Mountain sentinel;
With each season dons new glories,
  Yet the same old Mountain still!
So we see some lives about us
  Sweeter grow as seasons roll,
While beneath a changing surface
  Dwells unchanged a steadfast soul;

College Memories and Other Rimes

Staunch, unchangeable in duty;
Changing but with added beauty.

20. ANEMONES.

Before the warm sunshine has driven the snow
From hillside, ravine, and the slopes where they grow,
They come as a prophecy, telling of spring.
Ah! who can e'er tell how much gladness they bring!
What hopes and what promises bright seem to cling
Around the brief season these Esquimau flowers
Appear, and, in spite of the elements' powers,
Seem only to smile at the cold April showers,
Wrapt warm in their furs and all huddled together.
They herald, as forerunners, sunshiny weather,—
They herald its coming—but ere it is here
They've withered away; for they never appear
To share in the joys of the Springtime they bring:
Their mission's to herald; that done, they take wing.

21. THE ANEMONE.

It stood alone
   In yon ravine,
   Where all unseen
Its flower had blown.
        The March winds howled,—
         It did not stir,
         For all in fur
        'Twas robed and cowled.
At storm and cold
  And tempest wild
  It only smiled,
And spring foretold.
        No eye approved,
         None shared its lot;
         Yet—though forgot—
        It stood unmoved.
Brave little flower,
  Anemone,
  Impart to me
They gentle power
        To stand serene,—
         Though all without
         Be storm and doubt,
        Still calm within!

22. THE PINES.

The pines, the pines! I love the pines! Away
With weak, deciduous broods which faint or die
Of fright at every passing storm! Give me
The pines which stand unmoved, in verdure clad
The year around,—a pledge that winter's sham
Of death is but a sleep. Brave Optimists!
Not in the poison-breathing lowlands dank,
But tow'ring on the heights which cleave the skies,
They lift their heaven-aspiring pinnacles,
And bear aloft their rich Aeolian lyres
Which breathe, responsive to the breath of God,
Unending hymns, of majesty divine;
While earthlings, grov'ling in the depths and sunk
In mute and sightless discord, age and die.

Perpetual youth! Ye pines the secret hold—
A life in harmony with God, which breathes
Eternally in song!

23. TO SPENSER.

O Spenser, who did'st sing in former times
  The Truth, half-hid in allegoric phrase:
  Still, moved with wonder in these later days,
We feel the gentle beauty of thy rimes.
With thee we fly to quaint, forgotten climes,
  We pierce the dim mirage that o'er them plays,
  See knightly courtiers, hear the minstrels' lays,
And listen, rev'rent, to the sacred chimes.
  Thou clothest old truths in so pleasing guise
That sneering prejudice and doubt can raise
  No carping negative. With glove of mail
  Thou dost hypocrisy and vice assai'
Calmly thou stand'st, with Shield of Faith ablaze,—
And, smitten by its light, base Error dies.

24. TO BYRON.

No more with scourging condemnation told
  We bare thy vices to the curious crowd,
  No longer cry our criticisms loud;
Heredity and circumstance did mould
Thy life amiss. Thy passion'd measures, bold,
  Revolt against misfortunes which had bow'd
  A spirit less contained, obdurate, proud,
And which thy path in hopeless gloom enfold.
  Instead, we pity thee the dull despair,
The canker, worm, and grief which sapp'd thy youth;
  We mourn the wreck of pow'rs superb and rare,
Which might have served so well the cause of Truth.
  With mind magnificent, with senses keen,
  The Poet of thine Age thou should'st have been!

25. ON FRIENDSHIP.

O there are times when it is hard to bear
The wreck of plans which fail in spite of toil
And thoughtful care; when those we love recoil
From us, when those for whom we strive in prayer
And even popular disfavor dare,
For whom, unthanked, we burn the midnight oil,—
Seem from our very love to turn, and foil
Our fondest hopes for them; till, in despair,
The traitor thought steals subtly to the heart:
Why troublest thou for one who thanks thee not?
If thou would'st win him, to his standards bend.
But swift the answer comes: 'Tis friendship's part
To be, though only cold rebuff thy lot,
Still *true* to thine own self and to thy friend.

26. TO D. C. M.

Before me on my table
  A little frame doth stand,
And thou, O Friend, dost watch me
  From out its golden band.

So thou art ever with me,
  Though here or there thou art;
I see thy face, and bear thee
  Forever in my heart.

And daily as I watch thee,
  I raise for thee the prayer
That God may keep thee spotless
  In His protecting care.

Ah, sacred power of Friendship!—
  Thy presence, ever near,
Doth strengthen me in crises,
  My daily task doth cheer.

27. THE STRENUOUS LIFE.

Not weak submissiveness to fate,
But struggle, made our fathers great.
'Twas battling for each sacred right,
'Twas toil and pain and want,
That trained their moral fibre, firm,
Which hardships could not daunt.

The aimless ease of luxury
Robs life of half its powers;
The paths that lead to mountain heights
Are never strewn with flowers.

28.　GOLD OR A HUMAN LIFE.

Alone in a wretched hovel
　I found a miser old;
Unmindful of love or beauty,
　He cared for naught but gold.
　　　　Alone in a stately mansion
　　　　　I found a learned man,
　　　　A talented, wealthy scholar,
　　　　　Whose cheeks were sunk and wan
From luxury. Selfish pleasure,
　The quest for show and fame,
The gaining of ease and culture,
　He made his life's sole aim.
　　　　Unmindful of want and suffering
　　　　　Among his fellowmen;—
　　　　The poor and oppressed for succor
　　　　　Ne'er came to him again;
Unmindful of blind and groping,
　Outside in hopeless night,
From whom in his splendid palace
　He shut away the light;
　　　　Disdaining the lame and leper,
　　　　　Whose pain his skill could cure;—
　　　　His sympathy, cheer, or counsel,
　　　　　Ne'er helped a friend endure.

College Memories and Other Rimes

Ah, which was the greater miser,—
  The man who hid his gold,
Or the man who hoarded his talents,
  Whose heart was hard and cold?
        For out in the world of struggle,
          Where want and pain are rife,
          Which, think you, of greater value
          Is gold or a human life?

29. "WITH TREMBLING HANDS UPLIFT."

With trembling hands uplift,
  We humbly pray;
We tremble in the Night to drift,
  Yet fear the Day.

> We pray that we may see
>   Thy face, and feel
> Thy presence hovering o'er, as we
>   In rev'rence kneel.

Yet, as we pray, we quail
  Lest Thou should'st hear,
And, lifting from our sense the veil,
  To us appear.

> We pray for keener sight,
>   That we may thrust
> Beyond; yet 'tis not greater light
>   We need, but trust.

We raise our blind request
  As children weak;
O give us what Thou seest best,—
  Not what we seek.

College Memories and Other Rimes

30. THE CHRISTMAS GIFT.

I.

Oh, wond'rous Gift of Ages, God reveal'd
In human terms, that man might apprehend
Whom he, though conscious of Him, sought in vain
In earthly forces or the firmament!
We had not understood the angel tongue,
Nor borne the awful glory of the light,
Had God in all His grandeur come unveiled:
He could not speak to us, but in our speech;
He could not show us more than human eyes
Can bear. Nor were it worthy God to take
Some form of nature lower than the one
Most high that mortal mind may understand.
And so the Christ, the perfect Man, divine
In human, human in divine, was giv'n,—
The only revelation God could make.

II.

Oh Friend, who'rt conscious of my love to thee,
Although thou can'st not see or analyze,
In future years, beyond the mortal veil,
We'll see each other face to face and know

60

THE CHRISTMAS GIFT

As we are known,—as we may then see God
And understand whom now by faith alone
We feel to be.—But even now we have
The type of love express'd by these slight gifts
Which we, in memr'y of the Greatest Gift,
Upon His Birthday give to those we love;—
These tangible revealers in the terms
Our finite senses may receive and weigh.
But if thou seest in my gift to thee
But so much gold or beauty, which I set
As valuation of thyself to me,
And not the subtler meaning, true alone,
That in the gift I give my love, myself,
In form which thou can'st see and hold;—
Then is my gift but empty dust of earth,
Which thou may'st pawn for so much gold, and be
The richer for the bargain.

III.

So, Oh Friend,
Should we the subtler meaning, true alone,
Of God's Great Gift to us conceal and lose,
Were we in Christ to see no more than man—
The valuation of ourselves to God—
And failed to see that God has in the Gift

61

College Memories and Other Rimes

Reveal'd His Love, His Sympathy, Himself,
In form which we may see and know
And worship, while we follow Him to Life.

31. A PRAYER.

I.

Lead me nearer, Holy Spirit,
  To the Source of Perfect Peace,
Till full trust in Jesus' merit
  Forces fears and doubts to cease;
Far above all worldly worry,
  Quest of wealth and fame, and free
From Earth's shallow show and hurry,
  Let me, Lord, commune with Thee.

II.

Yet, while men from Truth are straying,
  While in any heart there's pain,
While Sin's pestilence is slaying,
  While one captive bears a chain;
While, in heathen darkness, altars
  To the "Unknown God" arise,
And the groping seeker falters
  Prayers of longing to the skies;

III.

While from Thee, through want of knowledge,
  Love of sin, or poisoned hate,
In metropolis or village,
  Any soul is separate;—
I would not, by ease surrounded.
  In the Holy Place abide,
Careless of the sick and wounded,
  Who unanswered wait outside.

IV.

No; I crave Thy gracious presence,
  Not to draw me safe apart,
But that I may bear Thy essence
  To the great world's aching heart;
That my heart, with Thy Heart beating,
  As Thou lov'st may learn to love,
And become a plae of meeting
  For men's souls with *That Above*.

「大学の思い出」とその他の詩
多くは『コロラド・カレッジ・タイガー誌』に掲載された詩

ウィリアム・メレル・ヴォーリズ著
（1904 年卒生）

———————

少々愚かな戯れの詩も
賢明な人々に観賞されることもある。

———————

1903 年　予約出版

序　文

　大部分は気晴らしのために書いたものであり、訂正を受ける機会もなかったので、以下の駄作詩が文学作品とは思わないし、文学作品であるという主張もしません。批評家には批判を差し控えていただきたい。この愚かな詩を書いた作者自身が、数年後に振り返った時、恐らく満足な気持ちにはならないと思うからです。

　この詩集の題名になっている最初の詩が、代表作と考えてよいでしょう。思慮分別が試みられている一部に比べて、三部の無意味な言葉の詩は、正にその理由のために、読者にはおそらく最も愚かな詩に見えるでしょう。

　しかし、この詩には聖杯より茶こしに似ているほど多くの欠点があって、台無しになっているが、それでも詩のどこかに僅かばかりの快活なところや、より崇高なものを連想させる気品や、あるいは少なくとも気鬱や消化不良に効く少量の強壮剤が染み込んでいるかも知れません。

　激励や援助、賛同などでこの小冊子の刊行を可能にしてくださった友人諸氏に、衷心よりお礼を申し上げるとともに、感謝を込めて献呈します。

ウィリアム・メレル・ヴォーリズ [1]

1903 年 5 月　コロラド・カレッジ、コロラド州スプリングス市 [2]

訳者注

[1]　ウイリアム・メレル・ヴォーリズ ; William Merrell Vories (1880-1964) の略歴は巻末を参照。

[2]　ココラド・カレッジ（The Colorado College）はアメリカ合衆国コロラド州　コロラド・スプリングス市に在る私立の一般教育大学で、1874 年に創立された。

67

目　次

口絵　「松の木林」　著者自身の筆による油絵（前掲）

1. 大学の思い出……………………………………………71
2. 園遊会でのルーベン麦わらの山………………………75
3. 反射神経作用……………………………………………86
4. ティクノー館……………………………………………89
5.「鉄は熱いうちに打て」…………………………………91
6. オランダ語に苦しむ……………………………………92
7. 正しいオランダ語学習…………………………………93
8. 真実………………………………………………………94
9. 乳牛………………………………………………………95
10. バレンタインの贈り物…………………………………96
11. 絶望的状況………………………………………………98
12. 1902 年 5 月 26 日……………………………………100
13. バスケットボールのポスターに………………………102
14. 春分の嵐…………………………………………………103
15. そして貴方の考えは……………………………………105
16. 感謝祭の悪夢……………………………………………108
17. 他の視点…………………………………………………111
18. 過誤と過失………………………………………………112
19. 山と四季…………………………………………………113
20. アネモネの群れ…………………………………………118
21. アネモネ…………………………………………………119
22. 松ノ木……………………………………………………120
23. スペンサーに寄せて（ソネット）……………………121
24. バイロンに寄せて（ソネット）………………………122

College Memories and Other Rimes

25. 友情について……………………………………………………123

26. D. C. M. 君へ…………………………………………………124

27. 仕事に励む生活…………………………………………………125

28. 金貨か人生か……………………………………………………126

29.「震える諸手を差し上げて」…………………………………128

30. クリスマスの贈り物……………………………………………129

31. 祈り………………………………………………………………131

William Merrell Vories の
幼少期と青年期の概略（訳者編著）……………………………133
訳者あとがき………………………………………………………139

1. 大学の思い出

I

思い出します　思い出す　試験の前の夜のこと
真夜中に　揺れる光が照らし出す　詰め込む頭や
うつろに見える本の文字　頭に巻いた手拭を
机に向かい読書中　時刻を告げる暗い音
未だ読んでいない本の　真新しいページを繰りつつ
既に学んだはずの課題を　今になって学習していることを

思い出します　思い出す　試験のあった教室のこと
張りつめて　心配そうな　学生たちの顔の列
大きく書いた黒板の　迷路のような象形文字
怖れおののく我々に　笑うがごとく指をさし
悪鬼のように犠牲者を　質問攻めで困らせる
怖い教授を思い出し　夜毎にうなされたことなどを

思い出します　思い出す　薄れかけた記憶だが
（詰め込みすぎた脳細胞　細かなことを想い出せないが）
丸憶えして詰め込んだ　頭捻って無意識に
走り書きした答案が　再試か　合格か　落第か
いずれになるか考えず　試験が終わって安堵した
ああ　私の結果は不合格だったが

「大学の思い出」とその他の詩

II

思い出します　思い出す　あの楽しかった教会のピクニック
男女学生が互いに相手を伴って　休日ごとに楽しんだ
月夜のこと　麦わら運ぶ車で遠出して　わらが崩れて道に落ち
その清掃に疲れ果てて　街まで歩いて帰ったことや
三十人以上の大食漢のため　素適な軽食と冷たい飲み物
バターパンをたくさん運んだことなども

山盛りの美味なサンドウイッチが　たちまち無くなり
菓子を十分に味わうには　量が足らなかったことや
イバラの茂みに引き裂かれて　傷を負ったこと
大小の昆虫が　レモネードやミルクの中で泳ぎ回り
蟻が忙しく動き回って　砂糖を盗ろうとしたり
バターを身体に塗り付けようとしていたことなどを

思い出します　思い出す　楽しかった山登りを
この拙い詩作の苦労より　足の痛みのほうがひどかった
道路とは名ばかりの荒地を行く時　乗馬にいかに救われたことか
我々は暗唱が苦手で　オースチン・ブラフ[1] の頂へ登ったか
を
それに私たちの皆が　いや大半が試験にしくじった時
いかに壮大なユート山道[2] を憧れの眼で眺めたかを

大学の思い出

III

思い出します　思い出す　野外の焼肉パーティを
体を支える翼もないのに　心が空高く飛んだ様子や
歌をうたったり　スピーチをしたことなど
たくさんの牛肉　パンプキンパイ　漬物やりんご酒
ピーナツやりんごなど　取るに足らぬ食べ物に思われた
ブランケット・トス [3) に群がった楽しみに比べると

思い出します　思い出す　空高く飛ぶとき
遥か下から見上げている人々の顔を
広々と見渡す眺めや
遠くの地上で点滅する焚き火の小さな炎を
すばやく急降下して着陸したり　また舞い上がったりする
確かにブランケット・トスは素晴らしい

思い出します　思い出す　あの有名なピアソンの山羊を
恐ろしい角の生えた頭が　私の体に襲って来た夜のことや
山羊の大声で鳴き喚くのが　私の震える耳には
暴風が近づくように思えて　全身が恐れおののいたことを
力強く角で突き上げたり　激しく頭で打ったりするのは
最強のボクサーが打つ強烈なパンチにも負けないほどだった

IV

思い出します　思い出す　今なお考えても心が暖まる
烈しい風雨に襲われたとき　私の人生に

輝やかしい希望の光を与えてくれたことを
愛と誠意と信頼を決して失くすことがなかった真の友を
他の人々が私を疑ったり　私の意図を誤解しても
決して甘い言葉で　私を欺くことがなかった真の友を

晴れの日も曇りの日も　私と苦闘を共にした真の友人たち
人を安易に褒めないが　進んで相談に乗ってくれた誠実な友人
たち
彼らの友情は　利己心や軽薄な気持ちからではなかった
私の長所や欠点を見出すと　最善へと導く努力をしてくれた
以前は真の友だちに憤りを覚えたが　今は憤ることはできない
率直な批判のかげに　愛の心が秘められていたからだ

思い出します　思い出す　感謝の気持ちで思い出す
軽率な生活や　狭量な考えに偏らぬようにと
忠告してくれた人々の温情を
彼らの友情の手本として教わったこの教訓を守っている
真の友人は　最も崇高な目的の達成を援助する人々であり
援助された人は他の人の真の友となって援助するにちがいない

1) オースチン・ブラフ：コロラド・スプリング市の峰のとがった
　　山を眺める高原。
2) ユート山道 (Ute Pass)；コロラド・スプリング市の西部にある
　　山道。
3) ブランケット・トス：数人が毛布の端を引っ張って広げた上で
　　跳びはねるトランポリンに似た遊び。

2．園遊会でのルーベン麦わらの山 [1)]

（ピアソンの文学会に捧げる）

僕が最近訪ねて行った
行き先は　そうと　何処だっけ
そうだ　コロラドカレッジだった
そこでは精神は知識で養い
肉体は食事で養う
僕は金に窮していたから
従兄弟に会いにそこへ行った
（僕が１ドルほど貰ったかな
でも　彼は都会で育った割には
あまり気が利かないと思った）
夜になると賑やかな宴会を開く
学生仲間に彼は入っていた
彼は僕を連れて行こうと考えた
僕は１セントも持たずに行った

そうだ　天気は穏やかだった
ちょうど幼い眠り子のように
空には雲一つなかった
春の訪れを告げる
元気な声が高まるのを
森の中でも聞こえるだろう
木々は冬の眠りから覚めたようだ
あちこちにクローバの群れが

「大学の思い出」とその他の詩

緑色に茂り始めていた
早朝から小鳥の鳴く声で
大気が波打つように揺れ
あたり一面が波立つ水面のようだった
大地の香りが良くても悪くても
そよ風が香りを振り撒き
好奇心の強い君を
捉えて離さなかった
君はしばし用事も忘れて
簡素な生活に耽った

僕は彼の勧めに従って
貸衣装の夜会服を着て行くことにした
（ああ恥かしかったが　素晴らしかった）
仲間たちは　僕のために選んでおいた
女の子を紹介してくれた
だが　皆は僕の後押しをしてくれなかった
彼女はＴ君が好きだったからだ

そう　晩餐会は８時に終わったが
しばらく待っていなければならなかった
９時頃になっていたに違いない
二人ずつ隊列を組んで行進した
準備室から雑用係り室と来賓室を通って行った
娘たちは並んで　我々が通るのを見ていた
（そこで彼女らは腰を下ろして、冗談を言いながら

園遊会でのルーベン麦わらの山

生意気にも　偉そうに僕を見ていた）
食堂へ入って行った
そこが狭かったかどうか尋ねたかい
そう　冗談だが帰宅途中にある
礼拝堂の十倍ほどの広さがあったよ
塔をべつにしてだが
壁は古い南瓜の絞り汁のように
あるいに　小川の傍の牧草地と岩山の間に
並んだタチアオイの花のように赤かった
それは本当に真っ赤だったよ
それに庆石が敷きつめられて　真っ白だった
そこには３０メートルもあるテーブルが置かれていた
本当だよ　それが見たところ　どのようだったか
言葉では言い表せないよ
幅も同じ程あった
もし、僕の記憶違いでなければ
娘たちは花束を持っていたし
一人ひとりの前にはバラの花があった
娘たちは微笑みながら長い列に並んでいた
煙突の周りに巻き付いた　ブドウの蔓のように

雌雄の牛を一対ずつ組み合わせたように
僕らは娘たちと組をつくった
男は皆スマートな娘たちを傍にして
娘たちの如才のない話に耳を傾けながら
彼女たちの食事にも気を配っていた
娘たちは３０人ほどいただろうか

77

「大学の思い出」とその他の詩

僕の相手は　隣にいる娘と同じくらい可愛かった
君たちがいくら頑張っても　彼女を怒らせる者は
いないと賭けてもいいよ
実際に珍しいほど美しい顔だったし
（彼女は料理上手なのかどうか疑問だが）
小さな色白の手と顔には
フリルとレースの飾りをいっぱい着けていた
彼女は一番可愛いい娘にも劣らず
天気や草花の楽しい話を元気にして
４時間たっぷり話していても　決して疲れなかった
彼女は驚くほど熱心に話していたし
話は誰にも負けない人だった
僕はすぐにそれを知った

そう　各々の皿の前に
食欲をそそる品々の
メニュー表が突き刺すように立っていた
一般のレストランのように
僕は何から始めてよいか分からなくて
僕の席の傍にいたウエイターに
落ち着いた口調で「一番評判の悪い食事の献立表を
持って来てくれ」と言った
「今　そうしようと思っていたところです」と
彼は笑いながら言った　それで彼は騒ぎを起こさない
人柄の良い男だと分かった

食器類の眺めといったら！

園遊会でのルーベン麦わらの山

ナイフにフォークにスプーンが何本も
同じ種類ごとに置かれていて
仲間たちは作法どおりに使っていた
それで　僕は最初にどれを使うのか
パートナーに尋ねてみた
彼女は「外から内へよ」と言った
その順序に従うように彼女は言われていたのだろう
それで僕は答えた　君が食べるように
僕も食べればいいんだねと

僕たちがすっかり落ち着くとすぐに
貝殻付きの牡蠣がやって来た
牡蠣は小さいが　厄介な吸盤にくっついていた
ちょうどトウモロコシの皮むき作業に
人々が押し寄せ
われ先に仕事を終えようと苦心する時の
トウモロコシの皮のようにくっついていた
一番ひどいのは
皿を持ち去るベルが鳴った時
牡蠣の半分しか食べないで諦めたことだった
（僕がその日に一番苦労した仕事だった）

次にコーヒーカップが配られた
（実際に予想外の品物だった）
最上のコーヒーがなみなみと注がれた
ポットが火の傍にあったように熱いコーヒーが
僕はカップを注意深く持ち上げて

79

「大学の思い出」とその他の詩

カップから皿に注いで少し飲むと
驚いて声を上げた
そこにはスープがいっぱい入っていたからだ
コーヒーカップにスープが入っているとは驚いた
とんでもない間違いではないかと思ったが
多くの人たちは
容器が足らなかったからだと思っていた

次には大盛りの魚料理が運ばれた
それは君も欲しがるほど美味しかった
でも骨が面倒で　君は思ったことだろう
時には人前でなければよいのにと

次の料理は「パティ」だった
多分君はその料理を知っているだろう
糊の小瓶の中に
シチューを詰めた　小さな円形のものだった
そこで僕は　スプーンを突っ込んだが
押し入れることができなかった
それは紙でできていたからだ
なんという変な悪ふざけだろうか
エイプリルフールと書いた紙を
学校の行き帰りにくれるが
宴会はどこにもなかったと聞いたことがある
そのような悪ふざけだった

それから何か飲み物を持って来た

園遊会でのルーベン麦わらの山

サーカスレモネードだろう
赤みがかった甘い飲み物でとても美味しかった
その味に勝るのは難しいだろう
ただ十分に濾されていなかったので
グラスを飲み干すと
フルーツの小さな粒が残ったり
口に入れると　喉に詰まったりした
そう　女の子が冗談に言っていたように
君は笑わなかったら　体がどうかなっていただろう
この面倒な飲み物をパンチと呼んでいた
その理由はフルーツの粒が喉に詰まって
胸を叩かなければならないからだ
でもそれは容易に我慢できるほどのことで
とても美味しい飲み物だった

ウエイターが運んできた皿の幾品かの中で
小さなうずらの焼き身が　僕は一番気に入った
これは見た目には素晴らしかったが
その夜は若鳥があまりなかったようで
怖ろしく硬かった　僕のところに運ばれたのは
小鳥の爺さんだったに違いない

その夜の鳥肉は
僕たち皆の好物だった
ウズラの骨がすべて炊事場に運ばれると
次の品は僕たちの胃を困らせた
チキン・サラダだった

「大学の思い出」とその他の詩

あまり酸っぱくない煮豆より
僕は雌鶏の食べ残したもののほうがよかった
でも　その時邪魔があって
食事と談話を中断した
僕はかなり満腹になっていたので
皆が静かになった時
僕は僕の女友だちの方へ向いて尋ねた
「いつまで続くんだろう」
すると彼女は言った
「そうね　私はもうすぐ終わると思うわ
未だ使ってないのはスプーンだけだから
それで食事も終りになると思うけど」

そのように思えたけれど
次に僕たちに出されたのはアイスクリームだった
（それは僕の好物の一つだ）
それは白かったが　ガラスのような
珍しい実物のチーズの小粒がいっぱい入っていて
シトロンの皮の味がした

いろいろな形の菓子があって
丸く積んであった
僕は遅れぬように手を伸ばして
いろいろな種類の菓子を幾つか取った
僕はなんとなく心が惹かれたから

テーブルの側に美味そうに積み上げた果物を

園遊会でのルーベン麦わらの山

僕らは見向きもしなかった
ブドウにも　ミカンにも　その他の果物にも
それで僕は女友だちに「あれを食べてみないか」と
小声で言った　すると彼女は答えた
「もうお腹が一杯よ　もう食事は止しましょう」
「リンゴをポケットに入れろよ
外で食べられるから」と僕は言った

ちょうどその時　ホテルの給仕が
最後に持ってきたのは
まぎれもなくコーヒーだった　本当に
今回はスープでなく　冗談でもなかった
何もかも素晴らしく美味しかった
僕はこんなご馳走を食べたことがなかったし
食べたくても　もう二度と
食べられないだろう
次はビスケットだった
僕の手が痺れるほど固かった
しかし　僕は思った
工場の不注意な労働者が
包装したが　そのことを忘れてしまって
何年も経ったものに違いないと
　すっかり干乾びて固くなっていて
大きな鋏でも壊われるほどだった
　それで誰も見ていない時に
僕はたまたま一個を床にすべり落とした
（床は前に見たようにきれいだった）

83

踵で踏み潰してすっかり粉々にした
それで　僕は急いでスプーンで叩いて払いのけた
たまたま僕が壊した破片を
拾い上げることができた
それを食べられるほど
柔らかくなるまで
コーヒーにしばらく漬けておいた

ああそうだ　もう少しで言い忘れるところだった
私たちの食事中ずっと
楽団が演奏していた様子を言うのを
団員には初心者もいなくはなかったが
まさにプロの人たちばかりのようだった
音楽は静か過ぎず　騒がし過ぎず
ちょうど夢を見るようで
一年中が五月の気候のように思えた
天使が翼を羽ばたき　飛び回るようで
話声もかき消されるほどだったし
曲にのって動いているようだった

その時僕たちは行儀よくしていた
楽団員たちが立ち上がって出てゆき
次に別の余興が始まった
スピーチ部門が始まると
兎を追う猟犬のように
笑いの渦がどっと湧いた
僕はこれまでその半分も笑ったことがない

だって僕はあまり笑わない性格だったから
その後何処だったか確かではないが
四人の若者が歌をうたった
すると講堂は拍手の音が鳴り響いた
彼らは更に一曲二曲と歌った
この僅かな人数に大きな歓声が上がった
彼らは力強いグループでもあった
そうだ　僕はすっかり時間の経つのを忘れていた
十セントで時間を過ごしてしまった
終わった時は一時近くになっていて
市街電車は夜は走っていなかった
でも月は明るく照っていたし
僕たちは二人ずつが
とても素晴らしい眺めを見ながら
談笑しながら
家路を辿って行った

それ以来ずっと僕は考えてきた
あの若い時の宴会が素晴らしかったことを

¹⁾　ルーベン（Reuben）はライ麦パンで挟んだコーンビーフと
　　スイスチーズとザウアークラウトの温かいサンドイッチ。麦
　　わらの山（strawstack）は多くの粗末な物の意か。
　　Reuben はヤコブ（Jacob）の 12 人の子どもの長子で、ルー
　　ベン族の祖。

「大学の思い出」とその他の詩

3. 反射神経作用

（心理学科 A 組に捧げる）

『モリア[1] の老松の頂で
フィン[2] 系ドイツ人がホップの実を摘んだ』
この単純な語句が私に与えられたのは
私が解剖学を学ぶのに役立つためだった
私の聴覚器官が音を捉えると
反射作用を波のように伝えた
最初は外転神経[3] が収縮して
それから動体視力が反応した
眼球が反射運動で動きを遅くして
視神経にその作用をさせた
こうして記憶は視覚によって
かなり援助された

味覚[4] と臭覚[5] は共感せずに
顔面神経[6] と三叉神経[7] を経て
反射作用が引き起こされ
感覚の作用が素早く働いた
呼吸器官[8] と消化器官[9] は
私の手に受けた衝撃を鎮め
血液が冷やされるまで
私の頭は冷たかった
脊髄神経[10] が機能を停止していると
その神経はこの作用によって衝撃を受け

反射神経作用

引っ張ったゴムのように曲がった
しかしこれらの大きな影響のうち
最悪なのは舌下 [11] への影響であった

この神経が振動し始めると
私の舌も速く動き始めた
『「モリヤの老松に」（一つ、二つ、三つ）
臭覚　視覚 [12]　眼球 [13]
「モリヤの老松の頂で」
感情や　三叉神経が──もう止めよう
これで一分だ』──でも私は続けた。
『「フィン系ドイツ人」──
顔と耳と舌の外転筋　このため私はすっかり
気分が悪くなった　彼等は何かを摘んだ
──迷走神経 [14]　あるいは呼吸器を─
そう　それが器官を正しく働かす方法だ

『「何か」──脊髄の──副神経
「ホップ」──舌下の──ええっと──そうだ
それが全てだ』──でも実にひどいものだ──
それに　私の反射作用を起こした舌は再び始まる
一日中私の意思に反して
反射作用で私はもぐもぐ言い続ける
『モリヤの老松の頂きで
フィン系ドイツ人がホップの実を摘んだ』
今では私は毎日このように困っている
私は哀れな男ではないだろうか

「大学の思い出」とその他の詩

1) モリア (Moriah); アメリカ合衆国西部ネバダ（Nevada）州の東部にあるホワイトパイン郡北部の荒野。

2) フィン (Finn); アメリカ、ロシアに居住してフィンランド語を話す人。

3) 外転神経 (Abducent nerve); 脳から出て眼窩に入り、外側の眼球直筋に分布する第六神経。外旋神経ともいう。

4) 味覚 (Glosso-); 舌の意味を表わすギリシア語から借用の造語要素、母音の前では gloss- を用いる。

5) 嗅覚 (Olfactory); 鼻の意味を表わすラテン語からの借用語、(名詞・通例複数) 臭覚器官、(形容詞) 臭覚の

6) 顔面神経 (Facial nerve); 橋髄から出て、主として顔面に分布する第七脳神経。表情筋など顔面の筋肉を支配する運動神経で、唾液分泌を促す自律神経や、味覚を感ずる感覚神経などに分かれる。

7) 三叉神経 (Trifacial nerve); 脊椎動物の第五対目の脳神経。延髄に発して、眼神経・上顎経・下顎神経の三枝に分かれる。顔面の皮膚などに分布して知恵をつかさどり、特に下顎神経は咀嚼筋などの運動にもあずかる。

8) 呼吸器官 (Pneumo-); 空気・呼吸・肺に関連して用いられるギリシア語源の造語要素。

9) 消化器官 (Gastro-); 胃の意味を表わすギリシア語から借用の造語要素。

10) 脊髄神経 (Spinal nerve); 背骨の意味を表わすラテン語からの借用語。

11) 舌下 (Hypo-Glossal); Hypo- は under の意味を表わすギリシア語から借用の造語要素。

12) 視覚 (Optic); 目の・視覚の・視力の、中世ラテン語からの借用語。

13) 眼球 (Oculi); 目・眼球の意味を表わすラテン語から借用の造語要素。

14) 迷走神経 (Vagus nerve); 第 10 番目の脳神経。延髄から出て内臓に分布し、声帯、心臓、胃、、消化腺の運動、分泌を支配する。

4. ティクノー館 [1)]
歌──（樂曲：寂しく）

I

それはキャンパスに建つ校舎の中の女王だ
その壁を見ると　いかなる思い出が生じることだろう
応接室や食堂　廊下　集会室
そして図書室──とりわけその周辺に

II

ティクノー館に足を踏み入れる時はいつも
夢の中のようで　精霊に取り囲まれている思いがする
精霊はクラスの祝賀会や盛大な宴会など
昔の楽しかった事の　聞き慣れぬ話を囁いてくれる

III

ティクノー館では男女学生はそれぞれ砦を持っている
また　その秘密の半分も話されていないから
彼等のキャンディやチーズトーストなどの話を聞いても
実際には　我々が知っているのは　あまり多くなかった

IV

我々自身が参加して楽しかった宴会のように

「大学の思い出」とその他の詩

昔の祝賀会の妖精のことを夢に見たり　話を聴いて
いつまでも思い出すことだろう
我々の親しい記憶の中にティクノー館がある限り

[1]　ティクノー館（Ticknor Hall）；女子学生数の増加に対応する
　　ため、1897-98 年に建築された 2 番目の女子学生寮。（前掲
　　の写真を参照）

5. 「鉄は熱いうちに打て」

今　ギリシャ語は恐怖であり
　　ラテン語は脅威であり
　　　　それにスペイン語は手に負えない
しかし　私が間違っていなければ
　　オランダ語に取り組むことほど
　　　　厄介なことはない
　　　　　　　　平素はイタリア語では２時間
　　　　　　　　　　フランス語ではその半分余りですむ
　　　　　　　　　　　　しかし　オランダ語といえば
　　　　　　　　大勢の学生集団が
　　　　　　　　　　法廷の裁判官と話をするのに
　　　　　　　　　　　　一日半でも長すぎない
十人の学生がともに
　　十時間学ぶとすると
　　　　（合計すると　百時間になる。）
でも　私には疑わしい
　　彼等が力を結集して
　　　　オランダ語を克服できるかどうか
　　　　　　兄弟たちよ　君たちが奮起すれば
　　　　　　　“団結には力がある”
　　　　　　　　　共感する心で団結して
厳しいオランダ語の長時間の授業に
　　諸君とともに反対して
　　　　闘おうではないか

「大学の思い出」とその他の詩

6. オランダ語に苦しむ

（また　ちなみにテニソン[1]の詩でも）

オランダ語よ　オランダ語よ　オランダ語よ
　　お前のことを考えると
心の内に起こる想いを　私の口から
　　言葉で表すことは　まずなかろう

詰め込み　詰め込み　詰め込みは
　　昔から変わらぬ言葉の学習だ
詰め込み授業から決して息を抜くこともなく
　　欠席することも　休日になることもない

困ったクラスの生徒たちは
　　丘に登って見守ると
ああ　打ち負かされた教授の姿と
　　静まり返った教室を見て喜んだ

[1]　テニソン；Lord Alfred Tennyson(1809-1892) イギリスの詩
　　人。代表作は「イン　メモリアル」(In Memoriam)(1850) で、
　　ケンブリッジ大学の親友の死を悼む哀悼の詩。

7. 正しいオランダ語学習

君はオランダ語で何か楽しめるかね
　一日に１０時間勉強しなければならない
猛勉強しなければ　この言語を修得する道は
まずなかろう　疲労困憊だ

翻訳が良くなるようにと
　何時間も費やして　汗水流した勉学のために
気持ちを和らげ　苦痛を鎮めてくれる薬がある
それは我々の立派な先生が去ってしまう時なのだ

この文化と趣味の豊かな言語を
　追究するために過ごす時には
勉学は多く　快楽も多く　無駄は少なく
そして　勤勉な生活が最良だ

8. 真実

あるとき愚かな者が
学校へ行かされました
知識を多少学ぶため、
彼の頭に詰め込んだ
思い違いを除くため
これは嘘ではありません
その愚かな者は
私だったから

9. 乳牛

乳牛は穏やかな生き物だ
　　乳牛は死んだようにじっと立っていたり
それぞれ静かに伏せていて
　　草の香りの呼吸をして

乳牛の上衣は柔らかく　なめらかだ
　　すべすべとして　美しく光っている
歯は白く　ミルク色で
　　角はネービーブルーだ

乳牛の脚は長くて上品で
　　仔牛の脚より優雅だ
笑うたびに
　　口は顔いっぱいになる

それでも悪い癖があって
　　草の芽を美しいうちに摘み取ってしまい
女生徒や兎のように
　　いつももぐもぐ反芻している

「大学の思い出」とその他の詩

10.　バレンタインの贈り物 [1]

穏やかな風が
林の中を吹き渡り
　空には星がきらめいて
私は独りでさまよい歩く
森の道を
　恋人よ　私の近くにいて

雲に飾られた空に
君の顔や　君の姿が
　映されているのが見える
「私のもとに戻っておいで
君に会いたいから」と
　打ち寄せる漣が呼んでいる

回転木馬の音や
陽気な歌声が
　遠くに聞こえる
しかし君がいないから
どの音も石油タールが切れて
　軋んでいるように感じられる

（石油タールはピッチのことで
昔の人が創った材料だと
　言われている）
でも　悲しいことに

私には喜びが感じられない

　君が遠くに去ったから

　1)　バレンタインの贈り物 (A Valentine)；2 月 14 日の聖バレンタイ
　　ンデーに異性に贈られるカードや贈り物。St.Valentine(?-270
　　頃) はローマのキリスト教殉教者。

11．絶望的状況

（復活祭 [1] のボンネット）

先日とても奇妙な帽子を見て驚いて
私は何か響きの良い詩か
格調の高いソネット [2] を書こうと机に向かった
今はその気はないのだが　私が言いたいのは
ミューズの女神 [3] から霊感を受けていた間は
その帽子が私の頭から離れなかったということだ
私は鉛筆を持って椅子に座ったけれど
（私はペンを使っても良かったが
いつ使い良い筆記具になるか疑問だったから）
帽子に文字を書き込む考えはない
婦人帽に木の葉の飾りを取り付ける時に
鉛筆の芯で汚すかも知れないからだ
君のために調子のよい冗談をしようと
燃えるロウソクの傍で私が座ったのは
インクの線を引いた良い香りの紙の上だった
しかし私の意図を曖昧にしてしまったように思う
あたかも斜めに置いた紙に凭れていたように
私には選び続ける目的があるように思えるのだ
これまでにも言ったように　私は椅子に座って
リズミカルな詩行を詳細に創り出す案を考えた
私のことばの倉庫は十分に満杯になっていたので
私はボンネットについて書き始めた
そこには素晴らしい詩行の密林が生えていた

でも実際には未だ書き終えていなかった

　　　　　　結びの句

あまり好ましくない批評が

不明確なことで私に浴びせられた

今回はもっと穏やかな論評を願いたい

1) 復活祭；イースター（Easter）、キリストの復活を祝う祭で、春分 3 月 21 日以降の満月の後の最初の日曜日（満月が日曜日なら、次の日曜日）に行われる。

2) ソネット；14 行からなる、イタリア起源の詩形。イギリスのルネッサンス時代（エリザベス一世女王の時代前後）にイタリアから伝わり、エドモンド・スペンサー (Edmond Spenser 1552 頃—1536) や、フィリップ・シドニー (Philip Sidney 1554-86) などが優れた詩を書いた。

3) ミューズの女神：ギリシャ神話の音楽、舞踏、学術、文芸などを司る女神。

「大学の思い出」とその他の詩

12.　1902 年 5 月 26 日

一面の曇り空から
幾時間も雨が降り続いた
あたかも誰かが
　水槽を覆したように
　　　　　　　　道路は水が溢れて
　　　　　　　川のようになっていた
　　　　　　春の装いをした蕾の間を
　　　　　　　水飛沫が迸っていた
　学内の公園に
新しく植樹された樹が
逃れるための箱舟がなくて
　最初の地点から
　　　　　　　10 フィートも
　　　　　　押し流されて
　　　　　現代の船団のように美しく
　　　　　　航行していった
　とりわけ酷い目に遭ったのは
ティクノー館で大勢が
並んで食事をしていた
　男女の学生たちであった
　　　　　　　12 フィート近い幅の
　　　　　　滝のように烈しい
　　　　　水の流れをとても
　　　　　　渡って行けなかった
　水の滴る小さな覆いの下で

100

1902 年 5 月 26 日

その学生たち男女が立っていた
4 人の勇敢な若者が
　彼らを救いに来るまで

「大学の思い出」とその他の詩

13. バスケットボールのポスターに

さあバスケットボール試合に
招く呼び声がまたまた聞こえる
群衆の興奮した叫び声の中で
４年生と３年生は
２年生と１年生のチームと対戦する
電気の照明で光輝き
煮物の湯気とトーストのように
熱気溢れる体育館が開かれると
流れ込む学生の群れを迎え入れる
木曜日の夜には　おそらく応援席から
明るい男女学生たちの叫び声や
各自のクラスを励ます声援が美しく響くだろう
この感動的な大行事を見逃すならば
１セントすら持っていないことを曝すことになる
常識のある人ならば　バスケットボールの匂いを
追い続けて止められないだろう
二人ならば25セントで行けるが
一人では15セントが必要だ
皆はパートナーを
連れて行こうとする
人生で立派に成功するためには
人は五感を養うように努めなければならない

102

14. 春分の嵐

三月十一日の朝のことだった
（七日が過ぎて　未だ日の短い四日目だった）
ぼんやりとした　ほのかな明かりの中で
見慣れぬ荒涼とした光景を見て
　私は体中の血が凍る思いをした

新入生組をやり込めるつもりで
（寒かったが）丘に立てた旗竿に
ビラを貼っていた２年生の女子学生は
脅すように大胆な態度で
　大勢を眺め続けた

美人の新入生代表が
キャリー・ネイション [1] のような態度で近づくと
断固と断って　応酬が始まった
状況は荒れて
　敵味方が入り乱れ始めた

ああ　このような奇妙な光景は見たことがなかった
私は驚いて　「これは何ということだ」と叫んだ
それはダンテの地獄界 [2] の一光景ではなかったか
いや乱暴な５年生と６年生の女子学生間の
　争いに過ぎなかった
　　[1]　キャリー・ネイション (Carrie-Nation　1846-1911)；アメリ
　　　カの禁酒主義活動家の一人。

103

「大学の思い出」とその他の詩

2)　ダンテの地獄界；イタリアの詩人ダンテ・アリジエリ (Dante Alighieri , 1265-1321)。彼の代表作『神曲』は地獄編、浄罪編、天堂編の三部からなり、詩人ダンテが救済を求めて地獄界、浄罪界、天堂界の彼岸の世界を旅をする物語詩。

15．そして貴方の考えは

昔、野鳥の森を散歩していた時に
たまたま樹の高くに奇妙な広告を見た
「職業飛行士で　空高く飛ぶことで有名な
J. バード殿の飛行のお知らせ」
私はとても驚いて立ちすくみました
幼い雛鳥は親鳥に教えられるものだと
いつも考えていたからです
そこで私は近くの松ノ木にいる老フクロウに
あの奇妙な掲示は何かと訊ねると
彼女は言いました　「私たちの町には
女子クラブがあるのよ
母熊は子熊の面倒を見てばかりいてはいけないのよ
クラブの気の合った仲間は一つに集るの
（あなたはそれを烏合の衆と呼んでいますが
私たちは同じ羽の仲間と呼んでいます）
羽毛の流行のような重大な問題を話し合うために
（それは私たちの種族の快適な住居を作る
巣の藁にするために　古い箒を探すより楽しいよ）
私たちには演奏者たちの　また歌手たちの
非常に優れた音楽家協会があるのよ
それに私たちの空を舞う会では
驚く程の飛行士になるでしょう
以前　私たちはあの高い峰のあたりを
毎週一度は一緒に飛び回っていたのよ
私たち鳥の共和国の政治でも

105

食物や健康に関する事柄でも
（朝食や夕食に一番良い種類の甲虫など
無学な初心者には知らないことがいっぱいです
種々の細菌や　恐ろしい害虫が
以前　私たちが巣に使っていたクズ箱の中に
生きているという事実などをね
その代わり　法律に従って役人に消毒された
藁だけを遣うようになりました
そして　著名な細菌駆除運動家の幾人かが
私たちが巣で孵卵器を使うよう求めてきました）
そのような奥深い研究を　母鳥は行っていますが
か弱い雛鳥は独りに残されることはありません
ああそうでした　昼も夜も守るために
私たちが少しの間でも外出する時は
子守りの鳥を雇うのよ
それに　雛鳥が飛び立つ時が来た時は
J. バードさんを呼びに行きます
彼の看板を皆さんも見かけるでしょう
私たちと同じように　彼は雛鳥を巣から押し出すのです
（そして実際に彼は適切な料金を請求します）
私はそれを聞いて　とても狼狽したことがあります
あたかも自然が朽ち果てて　木々が悲しそうに
枝を垂らしているようでした
山の峰が白布で覆われているように　雲で覆われていました
天空が地上の苦悩に同情して
雨の涙を優しく降り注ぎました
私はフクロウに抗議しようと口を開きましたが

そして貴方の考えは

彼女は私を嘲笑しながら　しかめ面して答えました
「文明開花が私たちに計画を教えてくれたのよ
以前　私たちは皆　異教徒だったがね
今は人間を真似ているの」

「大学の思い出」とその他の詩

16. 感謝祭 [1] の悪夢

（フィツ - グリーン・ホーリーク [2] への弁明）

暑苦しい真昼のこと
　　トルコ人が横になって夢を見ていた
激しい嵐をものともせずに訪ねて来た客たちが
　　枝を広げた椰子の樹と花の傍らで
主人と奥方と共に感謝祭の豊かな食事を
頂こうとしている時の夢を
夢の中で彼は人々が嬉しそうな眼で
　　彼の日焼けした胸や、
　　古今東西で最も誇らしい小鳥を
　　じっと眺めているのを見た
彼は食欲の旺盛な来客が彼の太って
重そうな体を賛嘆するのを聞いた
　　一時間が過ぎて　トルコ人は目を覚ました
あの心地よい夢が彼の最後の夢となった
目を覚ますと　来客たちを食堂へ呼ぶ
ベルの音の鳴るのがはっきり聞こえた
また彼が目を覚ますと　これらの人々の前で
　　肉切りナイフの非情な一撃の下に倒れた

集まった人々の目の前に
晩餐の名に相応しい料理が出て来ると
　　テーブルは歓声で包まれた
森や野原で採られた果物が

108

感謝祭の悪夢

丈夫な板も曲がるほどに盛ってあった
美味しそうな収穫物がいろいろと
　　ここに沢山あるのを彼等は見た

彼等は飢えた人々のように　よく食べた。
　　誰も彼も腹一杯に詰め込んで
すっかり平らげた　七面鳥は
　　肉がなくなって　骨だけになった
そして彼らが競って口を動かすのを
楽しみながら　長い間話が続いた
　　そして素晴らしい宴会が終わった
その夕べも遅くなって　休みたくなった人々は
主人の瞼が閉じられるのを見ると
　　休息処を探して　そっと歩いて行った

睡眠室へ来て眠りなさい
　　主人が初めて満腹したと感じたとき
主人の処へ来なさい
　　熱があって頭がくらくらするとき
深夜には涼しい睡眠室へ来なさい
眠れぬ人たちは　静かにしていられなかったが
　　鳥がいっぱいいる中庭を歩く夢や
　　　果物や木の実や　水が湧き出る鉢の夢に
　　　パイやプッディングやケーキにクリームなどの夢に
　　悩まされて寝返りを打った

　　七面鳥の怪物たちが互いを嘲り

109

「大学の思い出」とその他の詩

　　　幾本にも分かれた枝に大きくなって
枯れて地面に落ちた南瓜に
　　不愉快な口調で教訓を語る
勝ち誇ったものは夜遅くから朝早くまで
　打ち負かした勢力を思い続ける
　眠れぬ時に見る夢の中で　嘲りの言葉を聞く
　　　「親愛なる親切な友人たちよ　元気を出しなさい
　　感謝祭が来ますが　一年に一度です
　それゆえ欲しいものは何でも食べなさい」

　1)　感謝祭 (Thanksgiving)；神への謝恩の日。（アメリカでは）
　　　11 月の第 4 木曜日。
　2)　フィッ - グリーン・ホーリーク (Fitz-Green Halleck 1790-
　　　1867)；アメリカの詩人。

110

17．他の視点

浮浪者や酔っぱらい達の暮らしを見ると
　　私たちがこの世にいる間は
人に気に入られても　　この世を去った後には
　　タバコやビールの臭いを残していることがある

香りにも　おそらく別の香りがあって
　　それが広まり始めると
孤独で　思慮の浅い兄弟には
　　地獄への道を歩み始める者もいる

「大学の思い出」とその他の詩

18. 過誤と過失

（ロングフェロウ[1] への弁明とともに）

空中に「過誤」を撃ち飛ばして
それが地上に落ちて来ても　私は気にしなかった
それほど思慮がなくなっていたから
邪悪な行為を見ても　恐怖心も起こらなかった

私は「過失」を空中に吹き飛ばすと、
地上に落ちても　何処へ落ちたか知らない
過失の結果を突きとめるほど
洞察力が鋭く強い人がいるだろうか

ずっとずっと後になって　遥か彼方まで
「過誤」が増えているのを知った
「過失」は巧みな技のブーメランのように返ってきて、
私自身の心臓に突き刺さったのを知った

　　[1]　ロングフェロウ；Henry Wadsworth Longfellow(1807-82) ア
　　　　メリカの詩人

19. 山と四季

I

山は見張り番のように立っている
　移りゆく風景や季節にも変わらず
晴れの日も雨の日も野原や森林を守りながら
　朝の陽の光を最初に迎え
夕べの光を最後に見送る
　夜明けや日没の薄明かりの中に
平野や谷が山の周りに広がっている
　山は立ち続けてきたし
これからも立ち続けるだろう
見守りを決して止めることはないから

II

作物を穫り入れるのを見たり
　肌を刺す秋の突風を感じるとき
寒さが身にしみる白い霜が積もって
　夏の支配が終わったとき
ヨセフ[1]の多彩な上衣で
　よく知られたような
秋の華やかな柄のマントで
　起伏の多い肩を纏う
色とりどりの木の葉や草で作られた
その美しさに勝るものはない

III

しかし、厳しく非情な冬が
　　思慮を失くした人のように、
右や左を激しく打ちつけ　苛酷な寒さで
　　地球上の全てのものを　無情にも
枯死させようとしているように思える
　　ダイヤモンドをちりばめた
この上なく豪華なオコジョ [2) の
　　毛皮のガウンを着た人を
山は嘲笑するように　暑く思わせるが
吹雪が決して危害を与えることはない

IV

やがて、谷一面の木に蕾を付ける
　　春の季節がやって来る
荒涼とした冬の景色がすべて
　　新しく明るい緑色の衣に変わる
そして山は周囲の
　　新しい衣服を着た人々を見て
もっと季節に相応しいマントを山にも
　　早く作って欲しいと　自然に呼びかける
山の冬の衣服は色あせて
重さが肩にのしかかるから

山と四季

V

自然の女神は世界の織機で
　山の夏衣のために
様々な緑色の材料を使って
　紡ぎ　織り始める
女神の作業は静かだと言われるけれど
　忙しく響く音を聞きなさい！
小川のせせらぎに響く紡錘の音、
　小鳥の歌声に耳を傾けなさい
小鳥の声が聞こえ始めると
自然は糸を紡ぎ　機織りに取りかかる

VI

新しい創造は素晴らしい
　麓から頂上へと一歩一歩
雪解け地が高く高く
　昼も夜も登って行き
まさに天地の境界へと
　夏の緑の織物を押し上げてゆく
数珠玉のように点々と連なる多くの野草が
　華麗な輝きを眼前に繰り広げて
平地から遂には頂上に至るまで
最高の芸術品として広がってゆく

115

「大学の思い出」とその他の詩

VII

日中の時間が進むにつれて
　峡谷や山の峰は
それぞれの影が変わって
　いっそう美しく見える
朝日の輝きから
　夕日が沈み
あの格別に優れた王冠のために
　金色と深紅色の条光を残してゆくまで
そして夏の月が明るく輝き
様々な夜の美しさを加えてゆく

VIII

この見張りの山が絶えず変化しながらも
　変わらずそびえ立っている
季節ごとに新しい美観を装いながら
　昔から変わらぬ山が静かに立っている
季節がめぐるにつれ
　私たちの周囲に幾つかの生物を見て
心優しくなる　変化する表面下に
　不変の魂が変わらず住んでいる
堅固で　その働きは変わりないが
ただ美しさを増して変化している

　1)　ヨセフ (Joseph)；(新約聖書) イエス・キリストの母マリア

山と四季

の夫。ナザレの大工で、縞模様の上着を羽織っていた。

2) オコジョ (ermine)；（動物）エゾイタチ、俗に白テンと呼ばれる。毛皮は貴族の礼服や裁判官の法服に用いられた。

「大学の思い出」とその他の詩

20.　アネモネ ¹⁾ の群れ

アネモネが生える丘陵や峡谷や山の斜面から
暖かい陽の光で　雪が解ける前に
春を告げる預言者のように芽を出す
ああ　その花がいかに多くの喜びを持たらすことか誰が言えよう
このエスキモー ²⁾ の花が芽生える短い季節から
いかなる希望も　いかなる明るい約束も
いつまでも消えぬように思われる
自然の力にも負けず　四月の冷たい驟雨に遭っても
毛皮に温かく包まれて　群がり微笑むだけのようだ
アネモネは好天気の前触れをする
好天を予報するが　好天になると　花は枯れてしまう
アネモネが運び来る春の季節の喜びを
共に楽しむように思えないから　花の使命は
予告することで　それが終わると飛び去って行く

1) アネモネ (anemone)；キンポウゲ科ニリンソウ属の多年草の総称。春に茎が出て、赤、青、紫、白色など 3 〜 5 センチほどの花が咲く。
2) エスキモー人 (Esquimau , Eskimo とも表わす)；アラスカ、シベリア北東部に住む部族。グリーンランド、カナダ北部に住む人は Inuit, Innuit という。

21．アネモネ

それは向こうの峡谷に
　　ただ一本立っていたが
　　誰にも見られずに
花は飛び去ってしまった
　　　　　　　三月の風が吹き抜けても
　　　　　　　　それは微動だにもしなかった
　　　　　　　　毛皮の衣と頭巾を
　　　　　　　纏っていたから

嵐や寒気や
　　吹雪に遭っても
　　ただ微笑むだけで
春を予告していた
　　　　　　　それを見て満足する人もなく
　　　　　　　　運命を共にする人もいなかった
　　　　　　　　だが　忘れられてはいるが
　　　　　　　それは動かずに立っていた

勇敢で小さな花の
　　アネモネは
　　穏やかな力を
私に与えてくれる
　　　　　　　静かに立っている力を
　　　　　　　　外は全て嵐か
　　　　　　　　嵐のようであろうと
　　　　　　　心の中は静かであるように

119

「大学の思い出」とその他の詩

22. 松ノ木

松ノ木　松ノ木　私の愛する松ノ木よ
嵐が来るたびに　恐怖のあまり枯れてしまう
そんな弱い落葉樹は無用だ
一年中緑の衣を装って　動かずに立っている
松ノ木こそ望ましい　冬には枯れたように見えても
ただ眠っているだけで　勇気ある楽天家だ
湿気が多い　悪臭のする低地でなく
松ノ木は　大空を分かつ峰に聳え
大空に大志を抱く峰々を一層高くし
アイオロス[1]の立派な竪琴を　空高く掲げて
神の言葉に応えて　崇高なる神を
果てしなく讃美する歌を奏でる
人間は森の奥で倒れて　口も眼も衰えて
年老いて　亡くなってゆくが

永遠なる若者よ　汝ら松ノ木は秘密を持っている
神に従順に生きる生命の歌を
果てしなく口ずさむ秘密を持っている

[1]　アイオロス (Aeolian) の竪琴；ギリシャ神話の風の神アイオ
　　ロスの息吹で竪琴が音を出すと言われていた。

120

23. スペンサー[1]に寄せて

おお　スペンサーよ　以前は真実を
　婉曲な詩句で半ば秘かに歌っていた
　だが　近頃は汝の詩の優美さに
我々は驚き感銘を受けている
汝と共に忘却の彼方の古の国々を訪ねて行く
　我々は国々で映る薄明かりの蜃気楼の合間に
　騎士姿の廷臣を見たり　吟遊詩人の歌を聞き
聖なる鐘の音に謹んで耳を傾ける
　汝は古の真実の衣服を楽しそうに装っているから
　冷淡な偏見や疑問で欠点を指摘したり
良い点を否定することができないほどだ
　汝は鎖の手袋で偽善と悪徳を攻めたて
忠誠を表す栄光の盾を手に静かに立っている
やがてその光に打ちのめされて　卑劣な過失も消滅する

[1]　スペンサー；Edmond Spenser (1552?-99) イギリスの詩人、
　　代表作 The Faerie Qeene『神仙女王』(1590-96) はイギリス・
　　ルネッサンス文学で最も優れた寓意的ロマンスの叙事詩。

「大学の思い出」とその他の詩

24. バイロン[1]に寄せて

これ以上罪を厳しく咎めたて
　　好奇心の強い大衆に汝の悪徳を露わにしたり
　　声高く批判するのはやめよう
遺伝や環境が汝の人格形成を歪めたのだ
汝が激しい手段で大胆に抵抗したのは
　　自制心が乏しく頑固で高慢な性質を歪めたり
　　汝の道を希望のない暗闇に包んだ不運な出来事だった
それよりも我々が汝を哀れに思うのは
　　無気力な絶望や心の悩みとともに
弱気や悲嘆などが汝の青春を蝕んだことだった
　　真実の主義主張に大いに役立ったかも知れぬ
希にも優れた能力が損なわれたことを我々は悲しく思う
　　崇高な精神と鋭敏な感覚を持った汝は
　　汝の時代の秀でた詩人であっただろう

[1]　バイロン；George Gordon Byron (1788-1824) イギリスの
詩人、バイロン男爵 6 世（6th Baron Byron）で、バイロン
卿（Lord Byron）と呼ばれる。激しい情熱と奔放な行動の
代表的ロマン主義詩人。代表作に「マンフレッド」(Manfred
1817)、「ドンフアン」(Don Juan 1819-1903) がある。

122

25. 友情について

ああ　こんな時があります
細心の注意を払って苦労したにもかかわらず
計画が失敗して耐え難い時や　私たちの愛する人々が
私たちから去って行く時や　世間の不評を招いても
私たちが熱心に祈った人々や　私たちが深夜まで働いても
感謝もせずに　私たちの真心の愛に背を向けたり
私たちが彼らに抱いた儚い希望が挫かれたり
絶望した裏切り者がついには人の心の中に
巧みに忍び込もうと考えた時などです
どうして感謝もしない人のために悩むのですか
もし相手を打ち負かして　屈服させたいのならば
答えは速やかに出るでしょう　君自身にとっても
友人にとっても　やはり誠実であることが　君の運命には
冷たい否定であっても　友情を果たすことになるからです

26. D. C. M. 君へ

私の前のテーブルに
　　小さな写真の枠が立っている
友人よ　君はその金色の枠の中から
　　私を眺めている

君がどこにいようとも
　　君は何時も私と共にいる
私は心の中で君の顔を見ている
　　いつも君の声を聞いている

毎日君を眺めながら
　　神様のお守りのお陰で
君が無事でいますようにと
　　私は君のために祈りを捧げている

ああ　友情は聖なる力かな！
　　君がいつも近くに居ることは
私が危難に遭った時も力づけ
　　日々の仕事を励ましてくれるのだ

27. 仕事に励む生活

運命に弱く服従せず
　我々の祖先は闘って　立派になった
　苦難に挫かれることもなく
　彼らの道徳心を堅固に培ったのは
　各自の聖なる権利の闘いであり
　苦労と苦痛と困窮であった

　漫然と安逸に暮らす贅沢な生活は
　人生からその力を半ば奪い取る
　山頂へ至る路には
　決して花が満ちていない

「大学の思い出」とその他の詩

28. 金貨か人生か

みすぼらしい小屋にただ一人
　年老いた守銭奴がいた
愛や美に心を留めることもなく
　金貨以外に関心がなかった

　　豪華な邸にただ一人
　　　学識のある人がいた
　　才能は豊かで　裕福な学者であったが
　　　贅沢を知らず　頬がこけて血の気がなかった

自己本位の快楽と
　虚飾や名声の追求と
安逸と教養を得ることを
　彼は人生の唯一の目標にしていた

　　仲間たちの中の窮乏や苦難に
　　　心を留めなかったため
　　貧しい人々や　虐げられた人々が
　　　彼に二度と援助を求めて来ることはなかった

目が見えず　闇夜で手探りをする
　人々のことに心を留めず
彼は豪勢な邸宅にいて
　その灯りを消してしまった

126

　　　　　　　　　　　　　　　　　　金貨か人生か

　　　足が不自由な人や　世間から疎外された人を
　　　　その人々の苦痛を彼の技で癒すことができるのに
　　　彼らを蔑視するだけで　彼の同情や激励や助言などが
　　　　友人の忍耐に役立つことが決してなかった

ああ　いずれが立派な守銭奴か
　金貨を秘蔵する人か
才能を死蔵する人か
　いずれの人の心が冷酷だっただろうか

　　　困窮と苦難が蔓延している
　　　　この争いの世界で　金貨か人間の生命か
　　　いずれに大きな価値が在ると
　　　　あなたは考えますか

29.「震える諸手を差し上げて」

震える諸手を差し上げて
　　私たちは謙虚に祈ります
夜は夢の中でさすらい
　　昼は恐怖で身体が震えます

　　　神様のお顔を見るために
　　　　神様が頭上におられることを
　　　知るために　敬虔に膝まづいて
　　　　私たちは祈ります

でも私たちは祈りながら
　　心が恐れおののきます　神様がお聞きになって
私たちの感覚のベールを引き上げ
　　私たちの前に姿を現わされないかと

　　　私たちは力強く進んで行くために
　　　　より優れた視力があるようにと祈ります
　　　それでも私たちに必要なのは
　　　　明るい光ではなく　信頼です

私たちはか弱い子どもたちのように
　　勝手な頼みごとをします　どうか神様
私たちが探し求めているものではなく
　　神様が最も良いとお考えのものを与えて下さい

30. クリスマスの贈り物

I

様々な歳の人々への素晴らしい贈り物を
神様が人の言葉で明らかにされたのは
神様の存在に気付いたけれど
この地上や天空で捜し求めて
徒労に終わった人が納得するためでした
私たちは天使のことばを理解していなかったし
神様の荘重な栄光に接していなかったが
神様がベールを付けずに崇高な姿で来られていたならば
神様は私たちの言葉でしか話し掛けられなかったでしょうし
人の目で見る姿しか私たちに見せられなかったでしょう
人の心で理解できる最も崇高なものより
何か低い自然の姿をとられるならば
それは神様に相応しい姿ではないでしょう
それ故　キリストは聖なる完全な人の姿をされた神様であり
神様がなされることのできた唯一の啓示でした

II

おお友よ　私の愛に気づいている友よ
幾年か後に君とあの世で出会ったり　気付かなくても
私たちは互いの顔を近くで見会って　互いを知ることになるで
　　　　しょう
ちょうど神様に出会って　信仰によってのみ神様の存在を感じ

129

神様であることが分かるように
今でも私たちは　神様の誕生日の最も立派な贈り物を記念して
私たちが愛する人々に贈るささやかな贈り物を
それによって表わされる愛の形を今も続けています
言葉ではっきりと本心を言い表わす人々は
私たちの限られた感覚では重荷に受けることでしょう
もし君への贈り物に　金や宝石ほどの物が入っているならば
それは君自身に対する私からの評価なのです
曖昧な意味ではなく　ただ真実の気持ちで
私からの贈り物として　私の愛を差し上げます
君が見ることも持つこともできない形であっても
私の贈り物は地上の空しいちりに過ぎないでしょう
それを多額の金のために質入れして取引すると
もっと豊かになるかも知れません

III

だから友よ
もし私たちがキリスト様に人の姿しか見出さないならば
それは私たち自身の神様の理解によるのでしょうが
また私たちが生涯神様に従って行く間に
見たり知ったり　また崇拝したりする形で
神様が贈り物の中に神様の愛や恵みや神様自身を
明らかにされたことなどに気付かなかったならば
私たちに与えられた神様の大いなる贈り物の
微妙な意味を見失うことになるでしょう

31. 祈り

I

聖なる御霊よ　私を身近に導いてください
　　完全な平和の源へ
イエス様の恵みを全幅に信頼して
　　世間の悩みはもとより
恐怖心や猜疑心を無くすよう努めるまで
　　富や名声を追い求めることなく
地上の浅薄な虚飾と混乱から懸け離れて
　　どうか神様　あなたと話をさせてください

II

でも　人々が真実なる神様から離れて行く限り
　　誰の心にも苦しみがある限り
罪の悪疫で人が死ぬ限り
　　囚われ人が鎖に繋がれている限り
異教の暗闇の中に見知らぬ神を
　　祀る祭壇を建てて
手さぐりで探し求める人が
　　天国への憧れの祈りをつぶやく限り

III

また　良識の欠如や　罪悪への好奇心が

「大学の思い出」とその他の詩

　　あるいは　蔓延した憎悪が都市や村落にある限り
人の心は一つに纏まることはないでしょう
　　誰からも答えられることもなく
望みもなく　ただ戸外で待っている病人や
　　怪我人に配慮することもなく
安逸な暮らしをするならば
　　聖なる土地でも私は住みたくありません

IV

いいえ私は神様の慈悲深い霊を切望します
　　私を無事に引き離すためでなく
広い世界の人々の痛む心に
　　神様が実在されることを伝えるためです
神様が胸をときめかせつつ愛してくださるとき
　　私の心が愛することを知って
人々の心にとって天の神様との
　　出会いの処となるためです

William Merrell Vories の幼少期と青年期の概略
（敬称略）

〔誕生〕

ウイリアム・メレル・ヴォーリズは１８８０年１０月２８日にアメリカ合衆国カンザス州レヴンワース 51 番街 1044 において、父ジョン・ヴォーリズ (John Vories) と母ジュリア・E・ヴォーリズ（Julia Eugenia Vories）の長男として生まれた。

父方の祖先はオランダ系移民で、ジョンはミズーリ州セントジョセフで実業学校を卒業後、レヴンワースへ移り住み、簿記係として働く傍ら、第一長老派教会の日曜学校の図書部で奉仕していた。

母方の祖先はイギリス・ピューリタンの移民であった。ジュリアはオハイオ州ペインスヴィルのレイクエリー女子神学校で学び、将来キリスト教の海外伝道活動に従事したいと願っていた。彼女はジョンと同じ日曜学校で教師として奉仕していた時、二人は親しくなって結婚した。

〔幼小期〕

ウイリアム M. ヴォーリズは幼少期は病弱であった。腸結核を患って医者からも見放されたほどであって、小学校入学を１年遅らさなければならなかった。ただ彼は音楽に大きな興味を抱いていて、両親に連れられて教会へ行った時、オルガンの演奏や賛美歌の合唱に心を動かされた。

１８８８年にヴォーリズの家族はアリゾナ州の北部のコロラド高原南西端に、フラッグスタッフという新しく開かれた町へ転居した。転居の理由はウイリアムの健康にあったと思われる。

「大学の思い出」とその他の詩

　ウイリアムが入学したフラッグスタッフ・スクールは小・中学校共存の小さな学校であった。入学当初は木造二階建ての校舎であったが、在学中にレンガ建築の校舎が新築された。

　両親が中心になって、この地にフラッグスタッフ第一長老派教会が設立され、ウイリアムはこの教会の礼拝でオルガニストを務めると共に、キリスト教信仰を培っていった。

　また、この町の西にはロウエル天文台があり、彼はしばしば天体望遠鏡で素晴らしい夜空の観察をして、大自然の神秘な美しさに感銘を受けた。

　このコロラド高原のフラッグスタッフの町で幼少期を過ごしたウイリアムは、このアリゾナの山や谷など大地の美しさに心を奪われ、心身ともに健やかに成長していった。

〔青年期〕

　１８９６年にヴォーリズの家族はコロラド州の州都デンヴァーへ移転した。転居の理由は、ウイリアムはフラッグスタッフの町の生活で健康な少年になっていたが、この町には十分な高等教育を受ける学校がなかったためであろう。

　ウイリアムはデンヴァー市内のイーストデンヴァー高等学校に入学した。彼は音楽クラブの創立に加わり、会長も務めた。彼は音楽と共に絵画に興味を持っていて、これらが彼の生涯の力となった。

　ヴォーリズの家族はデンヴァー中央長老派教会に転入し、ウイリアムはここの日曜学校でもオルガニストとして奉仕した。

　高校在学中に建築に興味を持ったウイリアムは、１９００年にマサチューセッツ工科大学へ進学することを希望して、入学の許可を得ていたが、家庭の事情でコロラド・カレッジ

134

(Colorado College) に入学した。

コロラド・カレッジはコロラド州の中部、ロッキー山脈の東側にある都市コロラドスプリングスに在る。このコロラド・カレッジは小規模な私立大学ながら、キリスト教主義に基づく高い教育水準の一般教育大学であった。特に建築学には著名な教授が教育指導にあたっていた。

ウイリアムは将来建築家になることを目指して勉学に励んだが、心境の変化からか３年生から哲学コースに転科した。彼はピアソンズ文学会 (Peasons Literary Society) に入会し、英詩の朗読会や学習会に参加して、作詩の知識と技能を養った。また機関誌『The Tiger』への寄稿を続け、編集にも協力した。

また、ウイリアムは学生 YMCA（Young Men's Christian Association）に所属して活動するとともに、これから生まれた海外伝道学生奉仕団 (Student Volunteer for Foreign Mission) に加わって積極的に活動した。

１９０２年、SVM 第四回世界大会がカナダのトロントで開催され、ウイリアムはコロラド・カレッジ YMCA の代表として、またコロラド州の代表としてこの大会に参加した。大会の講演に深い感銘を受けた彼は、自らも海外へ宣教活動に赴きたいと願うようになった。

１９０４年６月にウイリアムは哲学士の学位を得て大学を卒業した。コロラドスプリングスの YMCA で主事補とし勤務した。この時、彼は学生時代に作詩した大学時代の楽しかったり、苦しかった思い出と、信仰や友情や人生観に関わる詩３１編をまとめて『大学の思い出とその他の詩』（"College Memories and Other Rimes"）として自費出版した。

ニューヨークの SVM 本部から、日本の学校で英語教師を求

「大学の思い出」とその他の詩

めていることを知らされると、彼は直ちに応募して、日本へ行く準備に取りかかった。１９０５年１月ウイリアムはサンフランシスコから船で日本へ向かい、１９日の船旅の末、横浜港へ着いた。東京の日本 YMCA 同盟本部を訪ね、任地となる近江八幡の情報を教えられた。その地は仏教勢力が強く、キリスト教伝道は極めて難しいだろうということであった。彼は２月１日の夜行便で新橋駅を発って、近江八幡に向かった。

〔日本での活動〕

　ウイリアム M. ヴォーリズが英語教師として赴任したのは近江八幡の滋賀県立八幡商業学校で、在学生３２０名のうち滋賀県内出身者が半数余り、残りの生徒は他府県出身であった。この学校は予科１年と本科４年の課程からなり、商業科目の教育のほか、英語や中国語の教育に力を入れていた。

　ウイリアムは英語の授業の後、生徒を集めて英語で聖書の指導をした。このバイブルクラスは好評で、常に５０名前後の生徒が出席し、最初の１年間で受洗した生徒は１９名にもなった。しかし彼の熱心な伝道活動に対して、近江の仏教寺院の批判が強く、１９０７年に滋賀県立八幡商業学校の英語教師の職を解任された。

　ウイリアムは吉田悦蔵、村田幸一郎の援助を受け、住民の労働と生活を確保する医薬品の輸入・販売会社を設立し、会社で働く女子勤労者が学ぶ学校をはじめ、幼稚園、小中学校、さらに高等学校を開校した。当時、肺結核患者が多かったため、療養所・病院を建設するなど、住民の健康と福祉のために献身的に働いた。

　１９１９年、ウイリアム M. ヴォーリズは一柳満喜子（一

柳末徳子爵の三女）と結婚した。彼女は『清友幼稚園』を開園し、同幼稚園の園長を務め、国際会議にウイリアムと共に出席するなど、彼の活動を助けた。１９４１年、ウイリアムM. ヴォーリズは日本国籍を取得して、一柳米来留と改名した。

　高校生の時から建築家になる夢を抱き、大学で建築学を学んだウイリアムは、アメリカから建築家ジョシュア・ヴォーゲル夫妻を招いて建築設計事務所の「ヴォーリズ合名会社」を設立し、関西学院神学館、同志社チャペル、神戸女学院、広島女学校、宮城女学校、ウイルミナ女学校等の校舎はじめ、京都、東京他多くのキリスト教会や YMCA 会館、大阪の大同生命、大丸デパート、東京の山の上ホテルなど、その他多くの著名な洋風建築の設計、建築にあたった。

　１９２０年ウイリアムと吉田悦蔵、村田幸一郎が資本金を出資して「近江セールズ株式会社」を設立し、建築関係の材料や薬品、雑貨の輸入と販売を行った。アメリカのメンソレータム創業者ハイドの好意でメンソレータムの日本や朝鮮、満州での販売権を得た会社は、鶴原誠蔵、木村巳之吉、竹内緑之助らの尽力で、販路が拡大されてゆき、１９３１年メンソレータムを自社で製造・販売するヴォーリズ会社を建設するに至った。

　ウイリアムは幼い時から豊かな詩心に恵まれ、両親の敬虔なキリスト教信仰に基づく養育と共に、自らもキリスト教教会や大学の宗教団体での活躍で培われた信仰心から、彼は優れた信仰詩を多数創作し、来日後に創作された詩は『東と西の詩集』"Poems of the East and West"(1960 年) として出版された。賛美歌 "Let there be light" は 1934 年版『賛美歌』に 236 番「神の国」として収録された。「同志社カレッジソング」"One Purpose Doshisha" の歌詞はウイリアム M. ヴォーリズの作で

「大学の思い出」とその他の詩

ある。

　ウイリアムは１９３０年コロラド・カレッジより名誉法学博士号を受けた。

　１９６４年ウイリアム M. ヴォーリズは８３年６ヶ月の生涯を終えて天に召され、満喜子夫人は１９６９年に召天された。

（訳者編著）

訳者あとがき

　ウイリアム・メレル・ヴォーリズ（William Merrell Vories）
先生は、１９０５年に英語教育とキリスト教伝道のために滋賀
県近江八幡へ来られて以来、キリスト教伝道をはじめ、建築設
計の事業に、病院医療奉仕活動に、学校教育に、また医薬品製
造販売にと幅広い福祉事業に専念されました。

　その傍ら、先生は詩作の優れた才能に恵まれて、敬虔な信
仰心に満ちた詩を数多く作られました。英詩集 "Poems of the
East and West" を『東と西の詩集』の日本語訳と共に 1960
年に出版されました。先生はコロラド・カレッジの学生時代
に文学サークルに加わって、詩作につとめられました。ユー
モアに溢れた詩や、真剣に人生を思索する詩などの作品
で、１９０３年に "COLLEGE MEMORIES AND OTHER
RIMES, MUCH OF WHICH HAS APPEARED BEFORE IN
THE COLORADO COLLEGE TIGER" の表題で出版されまし
た。

　訳者は２０１２年１０月に近江兄弟社財団組織の一つのケア
ハウス信愛館に入居してお世話になりましたので、ヴォーリズ
先生の人格と業績を少しでも学びたく思って、近江八幡市立図
書館へ通いました。そこには近江地方や近江八幡地域の資料を
集めたコーナーがありますが、その中にヴォーリズ先生の伝記
を記した書籍が幾冊かありまして、興味深く読みました。また
インターネットでヴォーリズ先生の事績を調べていましたら、
先生の学生時代に作られた詩集が販売されていることを知り、
早速注文して購入して読みました。その中には学生時代の様々
な行事や出来事などをテーマに書かれたユーモアに満ちた詩

139

「大学の思い出」とその他の詩

や、深い人生の思索と信仰を題材にした詩が、長編の詩や短篇の詩など３１篇が含まれていました。

　ケアハウス信愛館でお世話になりましたお礼にと、日本語に翻訳出版することを考えました。少しでも多くの方々に読んでいただければ、ヴォーリズ先生の学生生活や青年時代の姿を推測していただけるのではないかと考えたからです。私には詩才が乏しく、日本語詩の自然な感覚に訳すことができません。また私の乏しい語学力では難解なところも少なくありませんでした。ヴォーリズ先生が読まれましたら、君、ここは意味が違うよ、と言われたかもしれません。先生に代わって、読者の皆さんからご訂正とご指導を賜りますれば幸甚に存じます。

　最後になりましたが、詩の翻訳について村田辰夫梅花女子大学名誉教授に多くのご指導を賜りましたことに心からお礼を申し上げます。掲載いたしましたヴォーリズ先生の肖像、コロラド・カレッジの校舎の写真等は公益法人近江兄弟社からご提供いただきました。近江兄弟社本部事務局長の藪秀実様にはご懇篤な援助を賜りましたことに厚くお礼を申し上げます。この小誌の出版に多大のご尽力をいただきました英宝社編集部の下村幸一様に深く感謝いたしております。

２０１７年８月１１日

畠中　康男

《訳者略歴》

畠中　康男（はたなか　やすお）
1933 年生まれ。同志社大学大学院文学研
究科英文学専攻修士課程修了。
中高校、短大、大学にて英語教育に専念。
英語学習の図書を多数執筆した。

「大学の思い出」とその他の詩

2018 年 3 月 20 日　印　刷　　　　2018 年 3 月 30 日　発　行

著　　者　William Merrell Vories
訳　　者　畠　中　康　男
発　行　者　佐　々　木　元

発　行　所　株式会社　英　宝　社
〒101-0032 東京都千代田区岩本町 2-7-7
TEL 03 (5833) 5870-1 FAX 03 (5833) 5872

ISBN 978-4-269-82051-7 C1098
［製版：伊谷企画／印刷・製本：モリモト印刷株式会社］